Ordnance Survey Ireland

C000271822

# DUBLIN
## CITY CENTRE
## STREET ATLAS

# CONTENTS

## CITY CENTRE TERMINUS GUIDE
## LEGEND

**DUBLIN BUS**

CHANGING WITH THE CITY

# CITY CENTRE TERMINUS GUIDE

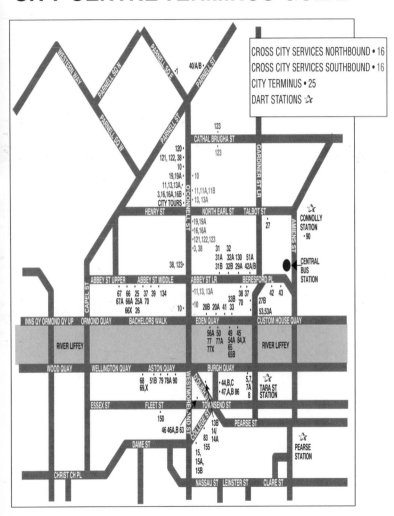

CROSS CITY SERVICES NORTHBOUND • 16
CROSS CITY SERVICES SOUTHBOUND • 16
CITY TERMINUS • 25
DART STATIONS ☆

WESTERN WAY

PARNELL SQ N

PARNELL ST

40/A/B • E

PARNELL SQ W

PARNELL ST

CATHAL BRUGHA ST

123

123

GARDINER ST LR

120 •
121, 122, 38 •
10 •
19,19A •
11,13,13A, •
3,16,16A,16B •
CITY TOURS •

O'CONNELL ST

• 10

• 11,11A,11B
• 13, 13A

HENRY ST

NORTH EARL ST    TALBOT ST

•19,19A
•16,16A
•121,122,123
•3, 38

31    32
31A  32A 130  51A
31B  32B 29A 42A/B

CONNOLLY STATION • 90 ☆

• 27

AMIENS ST

CENTRAL BUS STATION ●

38, 123•

ABBEY ST UPPER    ABBEY ST MIDDLE    ABBEY ST LR    BERESFORD PL

67  66  25  37 39 134
67A 66A 25A 70
66X 26

CAPEL ST

•11,13, 13A

•10

20B 20A 41 33

38 37
70

33B

42  43

27B

53,53A

INNS QY ORMOND QY UP    ORMOND QY    BACHELORS WALK    EDEN QUAY    CUSTOM HOUSE QUAY

RIVER LIFFEY

56A 50  49  45
77  77A 54A 84,X
77X    65
65B

RIVER LIFFEY

WOOD QUAY    WELLINGTON QUAY    ASTON QUAY    BURGH QUAY

68  51B 79 78A 90
69,X

D'OLIER ST

WESTMORELAND ST

•44,B,C
•47,A,B 86

5,7
7A
8

TARA ST STATION ☆

ESSEX ST    FLEET ST    TOWNSEND ST

150

46 46A,B 63

COLLEGE ST

13B
14/
14A

83
155

PEARSE ST

PEARSE STATION ☆

DAME ST

15,
15A,
15B

CHRIST CH PL    NASSAU ST  LEINSTER ST    CLARE ST

# LEGEND

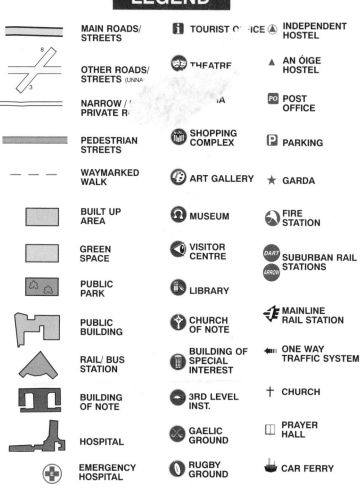

| | | |
|---|---|---|
| **MAIN ROADS/STREETS** | **TOURIST OFFICE** | **INDEPENDENT HOSTEL** |
| **OTHER ROADS/STREETS** (UNNA...) | **THEATRE** | **AN ÓIGE HOSTEL** |
| **NARROW / PRIVATE R...** | ...A | **PO POST OFFICE** |
| **PEDESTRIAN STREETS** | **SHOPPING COMPLEX** | **P PARKING** |
| **WAYMARKED WALK** | **ART GALLERY** | **★ GARDA** |
| **BUILT UP AREA** | **MUSEUM** | **FIRE STATION** |
| **GREEN SPACE** | **VISITOR CENTRE** | **SUBURBAN RAIL STATIONS** |
| **PUBLIC PARK** | **LIBRARY** | |
| **PUBLIC BUILDING** | **CHURCH OF NOTE** | **MAINLINE RAIL STATION** |
| **RAIL/ BUS STATION** | **BUILDING OF SPECIAL INTEREST** | **ONE WAY TRAFFIC SYSTEM** |
| **BUILDING OF NOTE** | **3RD LEVEL INST.** | **† CHURCH** |
| **HOSPITAL** | **GAELIC GROUND** | **PRAYER HALL** |
| **EMERGENCY HOSPITAL** | **RUGBY GROUND** | **CAR FERRY** |
| **WATER** | **SOCCER GROUND** | **AIRPORT** |

**SCALE 1:10 000**
**(1 cm = 100 metres)**    100m  50m  0 metres   100m   200m   300m   400m   500m metres

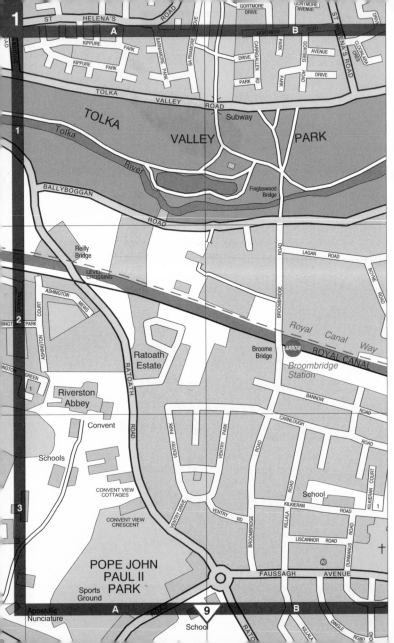

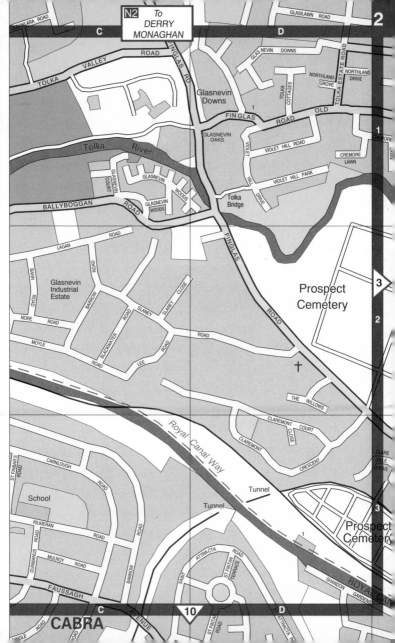

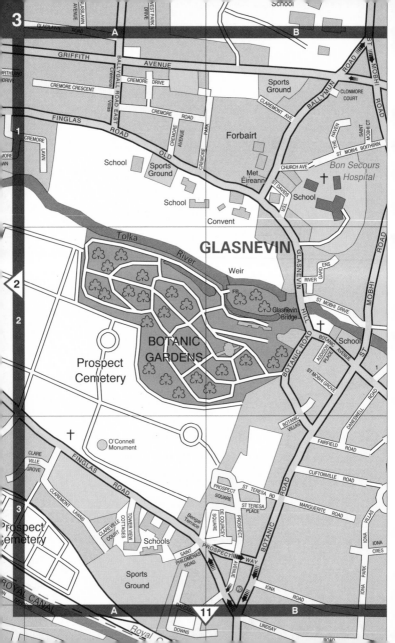

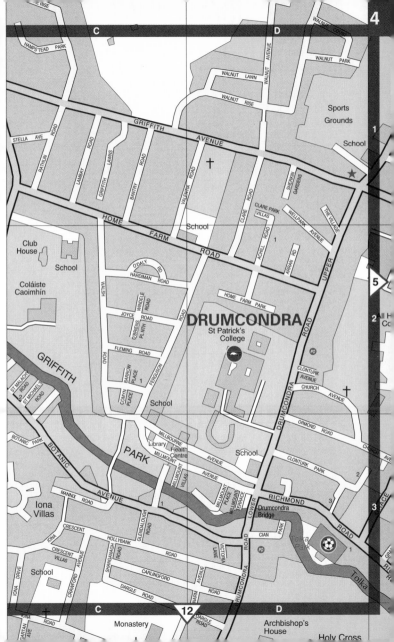

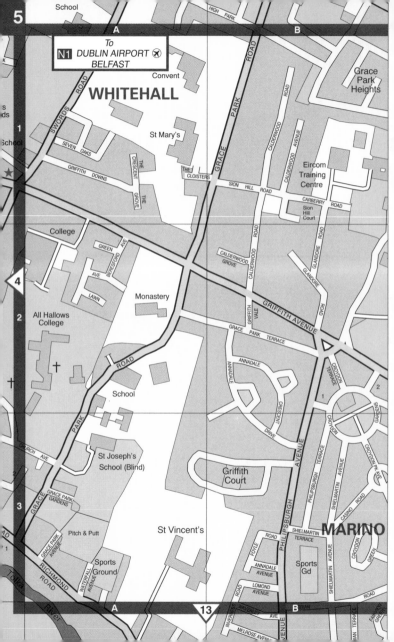

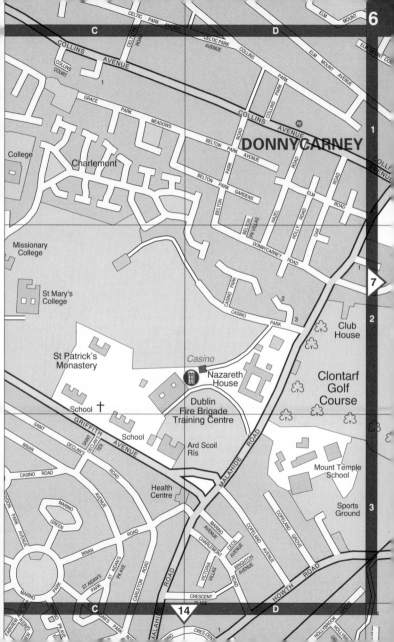

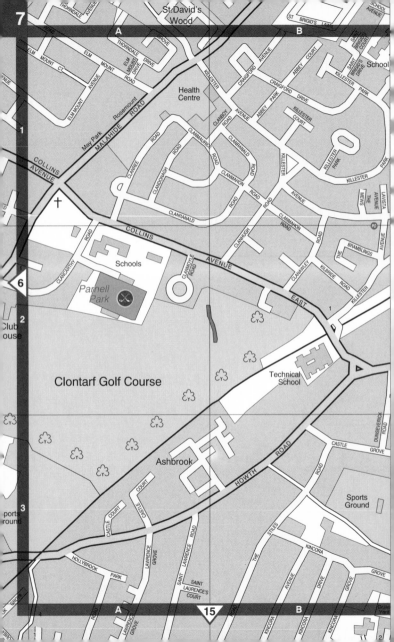

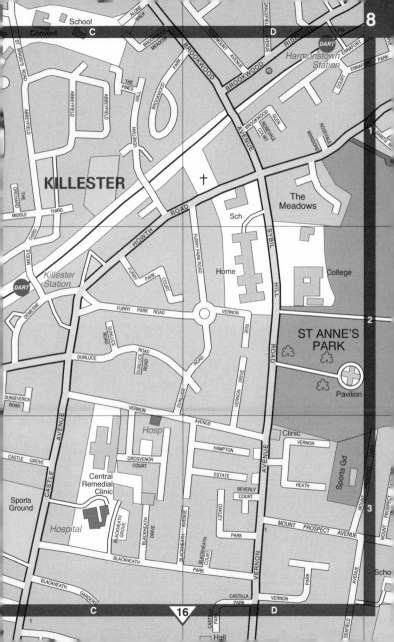

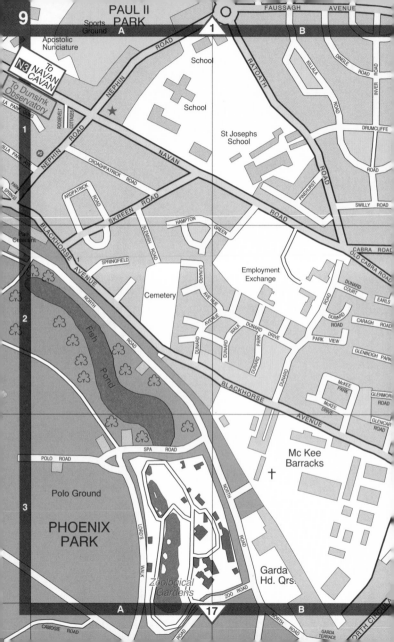

**9**

PAUL II PARK

Sports Ground

FAUSSAGH AVENUE

A

1

B

Apostolic Nunciature

School

School

St Josephs School

N3 TO NAVAN CAVAN

To Dunsink Observatory

LA PARK DNS

ROOSEVELT

VILLA PARK AVE

NEPHIN ROAD

CROAGHPATRICK ROAD

ARDPATRICK ROAD

COTTAGES

NEPHIN ROAD

NAVAN

SKREEN ROAD

SLIEMISH ROAD

HAMPTON

GREEN

ROAD

RATOATH

KILLALA

DINGLE ROAD

INVER

ROAD

ROAD

DRUMCLIFFE

ROAD

PINEHURST

SWILLY ROAD

ROAD

CABRA ROAD

OLD CABRA ROAD

1

PARK SPRINGS

PARK

Park Crescent

BLACKHORSE AVENUE

SPRINGFIELD

Cemetery

DUNARD AVENUE

AVENUE

GROVE

DUNARD WALK

DUNARD PARK

DUNARD DRIVE

DUNARD ROAD

DUNARD COURT

EARLS

CARAGH ROAD

PARK VIEW

GLENBEIGH PARK

Employment Exchange

DUNARD ROAD

NORTH ROAD

2

Fish Pond

BLACKHORSE

AVENUE

McKEE PARK

McKEE DRIVE

GLENMORE ROAD

GLENCAR ROAD

3

Polo Ground

PHOENIX PARK

POLO ROAD

SPA ROAD

NORTH ROAD

LORD'S WALK

Zoological Gardens

Mc Kee Barracks

Garda Hd. Qrs.

GARDA TERRACE

ORTH CIRCLE

CAMOGIE ROAD

ZOO ROAD

NORTH ROAD

A

17

B

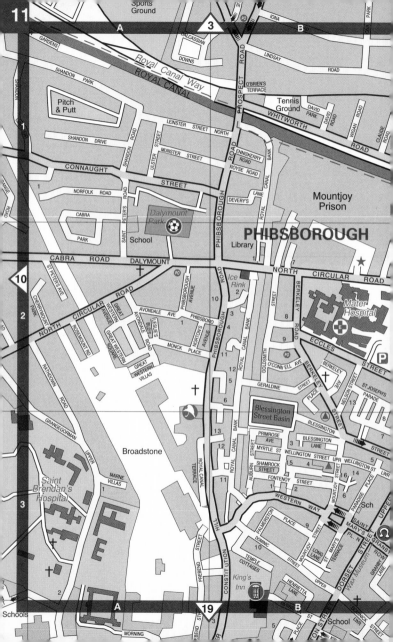

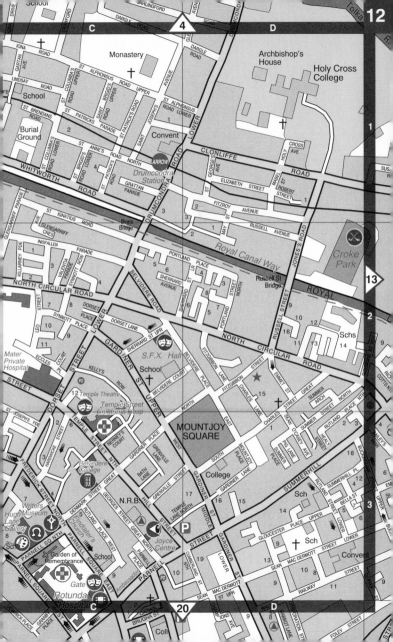

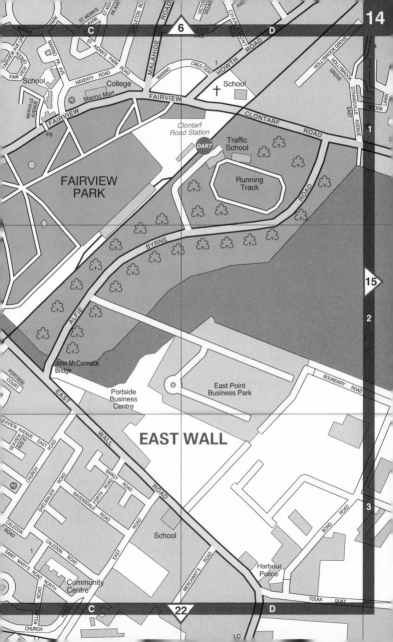

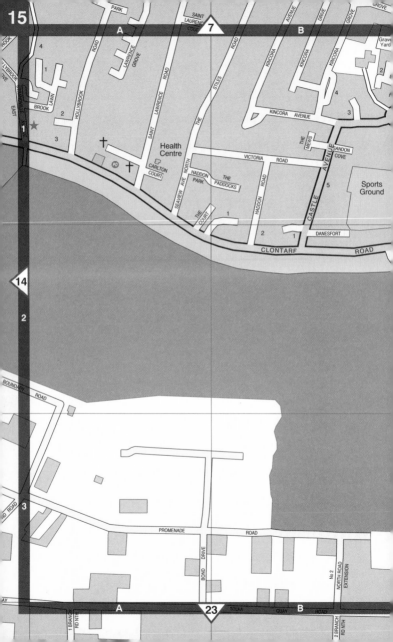

PARK

AVENUE

GROVE

A

B

Grave Yard

LLYBROOK DRIVE

HOOK

4

LAWRENCE GROVE

LAWRENCE ROAD

HOLLYBROOK ROAD

THE STILES ROAD

KINCORA ROAD

KINCORA GROVE

KINCORA DRIVE

KINCORA GROVE

1

BROOK LAWN

SHRUB HILL EAST

2

4

1

14

2

SAINT LAWRENCE ROAD

KINCORA AVENUE

3

1

3

Health Centre

PO

THE MEWS

CASTLE AVENUE

SANDON COVE

CARLTON COURT

SEAVIEW AVE NORTH

HADDON PARK

VICTORIA ROAD

HADDON ROAD

5

Sports Ground

THE PADDOCKS

THE COURT

1

2

1

DANESFORT

CLONTARF ROAD

14

2

BOUNDARY ROAD

3

ND ROAD

PROMENADE ROAD

BOND DRIVE

No 2 NORTH ROAD EXTENSION

A

23

TOLKA QUAY ROAD

B

AY

1 BRANCH RD NTH

2 BRANCH RD NTH

BLACKHEATH PARK

BLACKHEATH

C

D

PARK

AVENUE

SEAFIELD

AVENUE

1

CASTILLA PARK

Hall

SEAFIELD ROAD WEST

VERNON COURT

SEAFIELD ROAD EAST

Schools

MERCHAMP

VERNON

AVENUE

1

CHELSEA GARDENS

CASTLE ROAD

KINCORA

ROAD

KINCORA

ROAD

ROAD

BELGROVE ROAD

VERNON

KINCORA

VERNON GROVE

OULTON ROAD

CASTLE ROAD

Sports Ground

KINCORA PARK

VERNON GARDENS

Summerville

School

2

CLONTARF PARK

BRIAN BORU ST

1

BRIAN BORU AVENUE

CONQUER HILL

PO

CLONTARF PARK

CONQUER HILLIER AVENUE

Clontarf Baths

**CLONTARF**

VERNON COURT

FORTVIEW AVENUE

2

Toilets

CLONTARF ROAD

Yacht Club Slipway

3

C

D

TOLKA QUAY ROAD

WATER NORTH

NAL NORTH

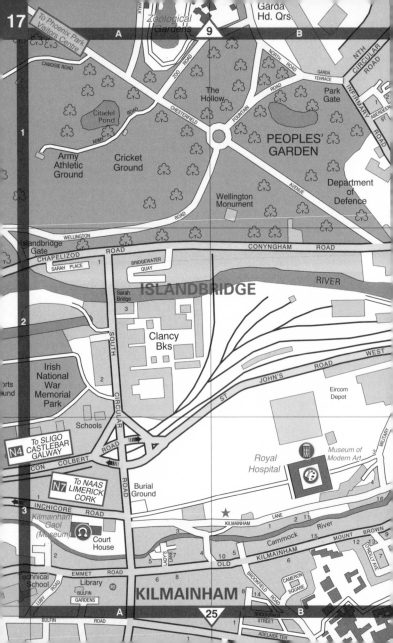

To Phoenix Park
Visitors Centre

Zoological
Gardens

A

9

B

Garda
Hd. Qrs.

CAMOGIE ROAD

ZOO ROAD

NORTH ROAD

NTH CIRCULAR ROAD

GARDA TERRACE

INFIRMARY

ABERDEEN ST

1

Citadel
Pond

ARMY

ROAD

The Hollow

CHESTERFIELD

FOUNTAIN ROAD

Park Gate

PEOPLES' GARDEN

Army
Athletic
Ground

Cricket
Ground

Wellington
Monument

AVENUE

Department
of
Defence

ROAD

Islandbridge
Gate

WELLINGTON

ROAD

CHAPELIZOD

SARAH PLACE

CONYNGHAM    ROAD

BRIDGEWATER
QUAY

Sarah
Bridge

ISLANDBRIDGE

RIVER

2

SOUTH

3

Clancy
Bks

Irish
National
War
Memorial
Park

CIRCULAR

2

JOHN'S ST

ROAD

WEST

Eircom
Depot

Schools

ROAD

N4

To SLIGO
CASTLEBAR
GALWAY

CON    COLBERT

N7

To NAAS
LIMERICK
CORK

Burial
Ground

ROAD

Royal
Hospital

Museum of
Modern Art

MILITARY

3

INCHICORE    ROAD

Kilmainham
Gaol
(Museum)

Court
House

KILMAINHAM

LANE

2    11

1

★

Cammock    River

15

MOUNT    BROWN

O'RELLY AVE

1.6

12

Technical
School

RUBY ROAD

EMMET    ROAD

Library

BULFIN
GARDENS

3

10    5

LADYS LANE

OLD

KILMAINHAM

6

BROOKFIELD ROAD

CAMERON SQUARE

8

14

KILMAINHAM

A

25

B

BULFIN    ROAD

BROOKFIELD
STREET

ADELAIDE TER.

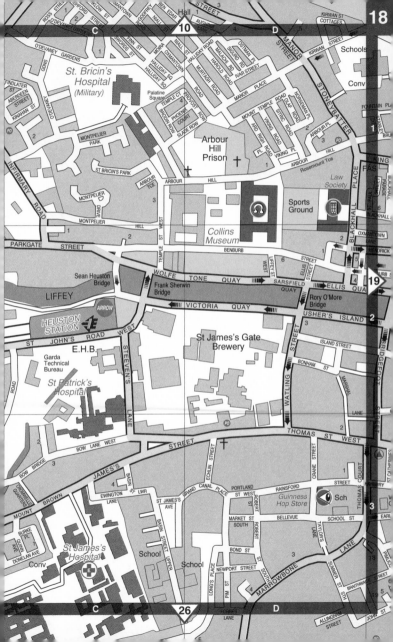

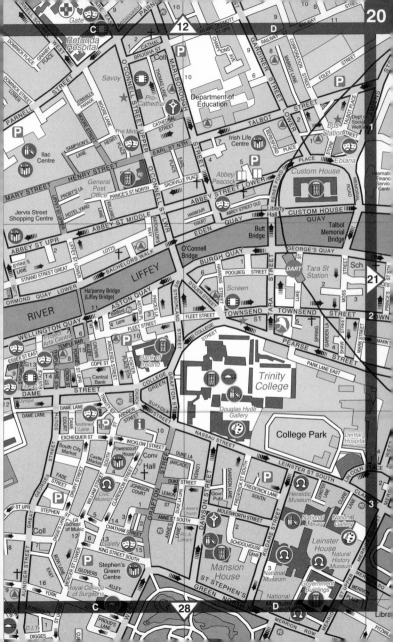

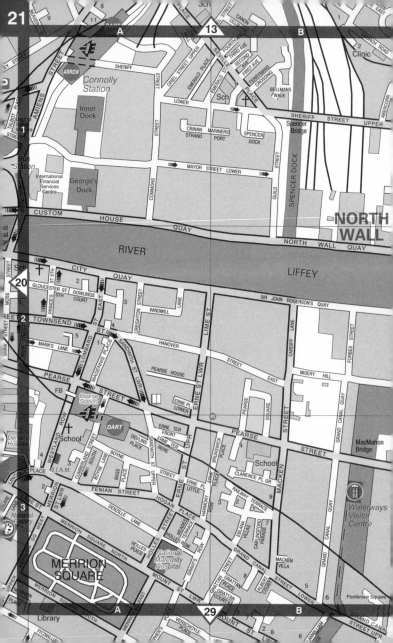

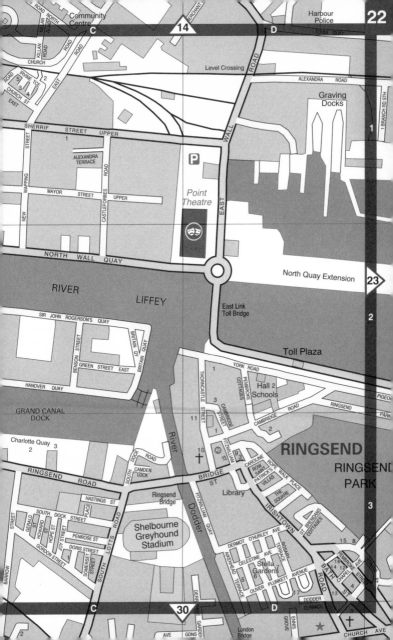

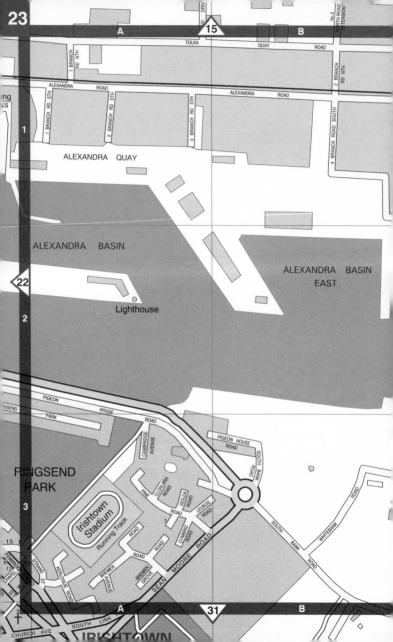

A
**15**
B

TOLKA                    QUAY                    ROAD

ND DRIV

No 2
NORTH ROAD
EXTENSION

1 BRANCH RD NTH

ALEXANDRA          ROAD

ALEXANDRA          ROAD

2 BRANCH
RD NTH

1 BRANCH RD STH

2 BRANCH RD STH

3 BRANCH RD STH

4 BRANCH ROAD SOUTH

ng
ks

1

ALEXANDRA    QUAY

ALEXANDRA    BASIN

**22**

ALEXANDRA    BASIN
EAST

2

Lighthouse

PIGEON        HOUSE        ROAD

GSEND        PARK

PIGEON HOUSE
ROAD

CAMBRIDGE
AVENUE

SOUTH BANK ROAD

RINGSEND
PARK

3

CLONLARA
ROAD

PINE

ISOLDA
ROAD

LEUKOS
ROAD

Irishtown
Stadium

Running Track

ROAD

ROAD

CYMBRIC
ROAD

ROAD

15

STRAND
ST

KENLOGUE ROAD

BREMEN
AVENUE

BREMEN
GROVE

SEAN  MOORE  ROAD

SOUTH    BANK    ROAD

WHITEBANK
ROAD

EMINGTON
CHAPEL

4

A
**31**
B

SOUTH    LINK

CHURCH    AVE

IRISHTOWN

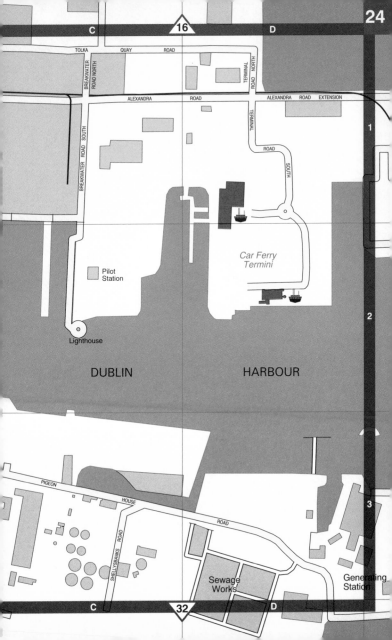

C

D

TOLKA QUAY ROAD

BREAKWATER ROAD NORTH

TERMINAL ROAD NORTH

ALEXANDRA ROAD

ALEXANDRA ROAD EXTENSION

1

BREAKWATER ROAD SOUTH

TERMINAL ROAD SOUTH

*Car Ferry Termini*

Pilot Station

2

○
Lighthouse

DUBLIN HARBOUR

3

PIGEON

HOUSE

ROAD

SHELLYBANKS ROAD

Sewage Works

Generating Station

C

D

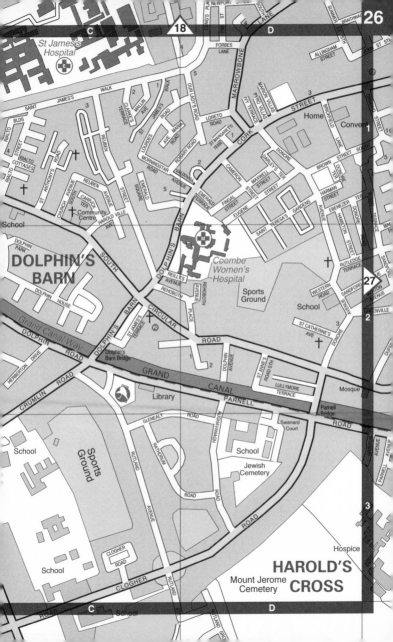

18

C · D

St James's Hospital

NEWPORT STREET

LONG'S PL

SOUTH

SUMMER ST

BRAITHWAITE

FORBES LANE

ALLINGHAM STREET

SAINT JAMES'S WALK

JAMES'S RD

MALLIN AVE

CLARKE'S TERRACE

OUR LADY'S ROAD

MARROWBONE LANE

MARION VILLAS

IVY TERRACE

PYRO VILLAS

CORK STREET

BROCKFIELD

Home

Convent

ORCHARD STREET

RRD

RIALTO BLDS

RIALTO STREET

RIALTO COTTAGES

SAINT ANTHONY'S ROAD

REUBEN AVENUE

JAMES'S ST

LOURDES

MARY AVE

MARY ROAD

LORETO ROAD

ROSARY ROAD

ST MARGARET'S TERR

CAMERON STREET

DONORE

BROWN STREET

DONORE

DONORE STREET

SOUTH

CONVENT

MORNINGSTAR AVENUE

VAUXHALL AVENUE

DARLEY'S TER

MAXWELL STREET

HARMAN AVENUE

EBENEZER STREET

DONORE

CHURCH AVENUE

REUBEN STREET

EMERALD SQUARE

EMERALD TERRACE

FINGAL STREET

EUGENE STREET

SAINT TERESA'S GARDENS

HAMPTON STREET

School

CARRICK TER

Community Centre

HAROLD VILLE AVE

SOUTH

DOLPHIN'S BARN

DOLPHIN'S BARN

DOLPHIN PARK

DOLPHIN HOUSE

DOLPHIN ROAD

Grand Canal Way

HERBERTON DRIVE

CRUMLIN ROAD

DOLPHIN ROAD

DOLPHIN'S BARN ROAD

REILLY'S

REHOBOTH AVENUE

REHOBOTH PLACE

ST JAMES'S TERRACE

CIRCULAR ROAD

Dolphin's Barn Bridge

Coombe Women's Hospital

Sports Ground

School

WESTERN ROAD

SANDFORD AVENUE

ST CATHERINE'S AVE

RUTLEDGE TERRACE

GREENVILLE TERRACE

SANDFORD

27

2

GRAND CANAL

PARNELL ROAD

DOLPHIN AVENUE

ST ANNE'S ROAD STH

LULLYMORE TERRACE

Mosque

Parnell Bridge

PARNELL ROAD

Library

GLENEALY ROAD

RATHDRUM ROAD

AUGHNAMAS

School

Swanard Court

GVD

Sports Ground

School

School

RUTLAND AVENUE

RATHDRUM ROAD

GVD ROAD

Jewish Cemetery

School

CLOGHER ROAD

CLOGHER ROAD

RUTLAND AVENUE

School

ARBUTUS AVENUE

PARNELL AVENUE

Hospice

3

HAROLD'S CROSS

Mount Jerome Cemetery

C · D

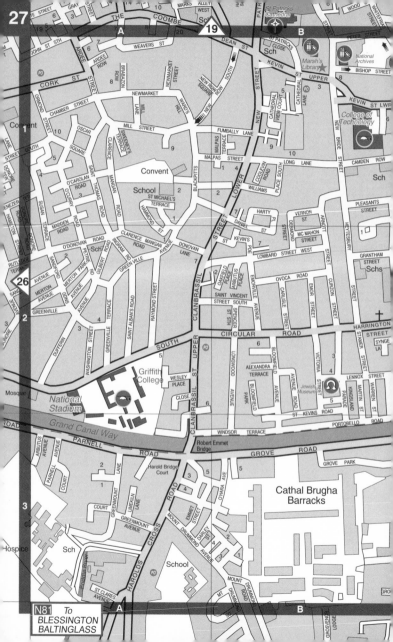

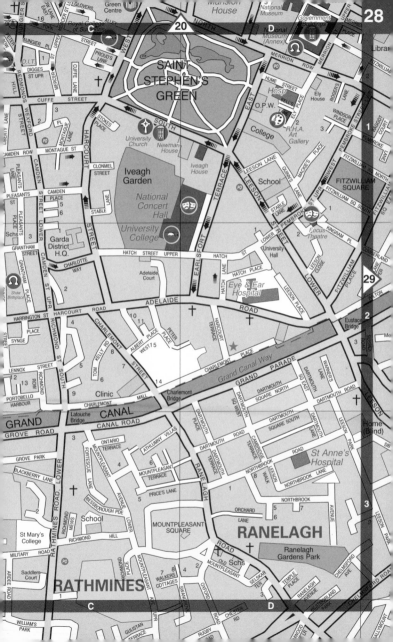

IRISHTOWN

NATURE PARK

1

2

3

Martello
Tower

# TOURIST INFORMATION
## Buildings of Note

**Bank of Ireland (Former Parliament House)**
**College Green**
Designed by Sir Edward Lovett Pearce and built between 1729 and 1739. Enlarged by James Gandon and Robert Parke between 1785 and 1794. The Bank of Ireland took over this building in 1804. It had been the scene of many dramatic events in Irish politics up to the passing of the Act of Union in 1800.
**Visiting Times:**
Mon, Tues, Wed, Fri
10a.m. - 4p.m.
Thurs 10a.m. - 5p.m.          **20 C2**

**Belvedere House/Belvedere College**
**Great Denmark Street**
Built in 1775 for George Rochford Lord Belvedere. It was bought in 1841 by the Jesuits for use as a boys college. The building contains some fine plasterwork by Michael Stapleton and fireplaces by the Venetian Bossi.
                              **12 C3**

**Bluecoat School**
**Blackhall Place**
Designed by Thomas Ivory and built in the palladian style between 1773 and 1783. The Interior has some fine plasterwork by Charles Thorp. The cupola was added in 1904. It is now the home of the Incorporated Law Society.          **18 D1**

**Brazen Head**
**Lower Bridge Street**
This is Dublin's oldest hostelery built in 1666. Its foundations which are at a lower level than the surrounding area suggest that it was built on a much older site probably Viking. Its was frequented by many Irish patriots including Wolfe Tone, Robert Emmet and Daniel O'Connell.
                              **19 A2**

**Casino Marino**
**Malahide Road**
Located 4kms from the city centre off the Malahide Road. The Casino was built in 1758 for Lord Charlemont from a design by Sir William Chambers. It has been described as one of the finest 18th century classical buildings in Ireland. Access is by guided tour only
**Visiting Times:**
**June - Sept**
9.30a.m. - 6.30p.m. Daily
**October and May**
10a.m. - 5p.m. Daily
**November**
12 noon - 4p.m. Thurs and Sat
**Feb-April**
12 noon - 4p.m. Thurs and Sat
Closed Dec - Jan.
                              **6 D2**

Casino Marino

## City Hall
### Lord Edward Street
Formerly the Royal Exchange, designed by Thomas Cooley and completed between 1769 and 1779.
This is the headquarters for Dublin's Municipal Government. Archives dating back to the 12th Century are stored in the Muniment Room. It also houses the mace and sword of the city along with 102 Royal Charters.
**Visiting Times:**
Closed due to restoration work. Opening in the year 2000.                    19 **B2**

## The Royal College of Surgeons,
### St Stephen's Green West.
Designed by William Murray and built between 1825 to 1827. It was occupied by the Irish Citizen Army during the 1916 Rising under the command of Countess Markievicz.                    20 **C3**

## The Customs House
### Custom House Quay
Designed by James Gandon and built between 1781 and 1791. The building was gutted by fire during the War of Independence. It was restored by the Office of Public Works after the Irish Free State was established.                    20 **D1**

## Dublin Castle
Built at the behest of King John in 1204 on a site which was once a Viking strong-hold. It has served as a military fortress, prison, courts of law and the core of British Administration in Ireland until 1922. The Castle is now used for State functions. Guided tours of the State Apartments, Chapel Royal and Undercroft.
**Visiting Times:**
Mon - Fri 10a.m. - 5p.m.
Sat/Sun/Public Holidays 2 - 5p.m.  19 **B3**

## General Post Office
### O'Connell Street
Designed by Francis Johnston and built between 1814 and 1818.
The GPO became the focal point of the 1916 Insurrection and the Proclamation of the Irish Republic took place there.
Destroyed by fire, it was restored in 1929. In the publc office is a noteworthy statue representing the Death of Cuchulainn, the work of Oliver Sheppard R.H.A.     20 **C1**

## The Four Courts
### Inns Quay
Built between 1785 and 1802 this is one of designer James Gandon's master-pieces. It houses the Irish Law Courts and Law Library. Destroyed by fire in 1922 it was completely restored in 1932.  19 **B2**

Dublin Castle

**Government Buildings,**
**Upper Merrion Street**
This building was designed as the Royal College of Science by Sir Aston Webb. It was opened by King George V on his visit in 1911. The Taoiseach's and some other ministerial offices are located here.

20 **D3**

**Iveagh House,**
**St Stephen's Green.**
This building built in 1736 was presented to the Irish Nation in 1939 by the 2nd Earl Iveagh. It is now occupied by the Department of Foreign Affairs.

28 **D1**

**Kilmainham Gaol**
**Inchicore Road**
One of the largest decommissioned jails in Europe, it played its part in some of the most partriotic and tragic episodes that light the path of Ireland's journey to modern nationhood, from the 1780s to 1924. Featuring many exhibitions and a multi-lingual audio-visual show. Access by guided tour only.
**Visiting Times:**
**Oct - March**
Mon - Fri 9.30a.m. - 5p.m.
Sun 10a.m. - 6p.m.
**April - Sept**
9.30a.m. - 6p.m. Daily
Last admission one hour before closing

17 **A3**

**Kings Inn**
**Constitution Hill**
Designed partly by James Gandon and built between 1795 and 1817. The Library contains 100,000 volumes including most of the Dublin directories published and a fine collection of English county histories. Not open to the public.

11 **B3**

**Leinster House**
**Kildare Street**
Designed by Richard Cassells this fine Georgian town house was built for the Duke of Leinster. The Royal Dublin Society occupied it until 1922 when it was purchased by the Irish Free State. Since 1922 it has served as a Parliament House which is the meeting place of the Dail (Chamber of Deputies) and Seanad (Senate).

20 **D3**

**The Mansion House**
**Dawson Street**
This Queen Anne style house designed by Joshua Dawson was built in 1710. The round room was added in 1821. It has been the official residence of Dublin's Lord Mayors since 1715. The Anglo-Irish truce was signed here in 1921.

20 **D3**

**Newman House**
**85 - 86 St Stephen's Green.**
The Catholic University (now U.C.D.) founded here by Cardinal Newman. The poet Gerard Manley Hopkins was professor of Greek here while James Joyce and Flann O'Brien studied here.
These two fine 18th century houses have been restored and are open to the public.

28 **C1**

Georgian Door

"Number 29"
Lower Fitzwilliam Street
Situated on the corner of Mount Street
and Fitzwilliam Street. This typical middle-
class home of the period 1790 - 1820 is
faithfully restored and furnished.
**Visiting Times:**
Tues - Sat 10a.m. - 5p.m.
Sunday 2p.m. - 5p.m.
Closed Monday					29 **A1**

Powerscourt House
South William Street
Designed by Robert Mack for Viscount
Powerscourt and built between 1771 and
1774. It is now a shopping mall including
cafes, restaurants, crafts and antiques.
					20 **C3**

The Rotunda Hospital
Parnell Square
The Rotunda Hospital was the first
purpose built maternity hospital in the
British Isles. Designed by Richard
Bassels it was opened in 1757. A feature
of the building is its chapel with its fine
baroque plasterwork by Bartholomew
Cranmillion.				20 **C1**

Royal Hospital and Irish Museum of
Modern Art
Military Road, Kilmainham
This the most important 17th century
building in Ireland has recently been
restored. Guided tours available of the
Master's Quarters, the Great Hall with the
portrait collection, and the chapel which
contains outstanding woodcarving by
Tabary and a magnificent Baroque ceil-
ing. The Irish Museum of Modern Art was
established in 1991 and exhibits Irish and
International art of the 20th century

**Visiting Times:**
Tues - Sat 10a.m. - 5.30p.m.
Sundays and Bank Holidays 12 noon -
5.30p.m.
Closed Monday				17 **B3**

The Shaw Birthplace
Synge Street
Situated at No. 33 Synge Street this is the
birthplace of George Bernard Shaw the
Nobel prizewinning author and play-
wright. Built in 1838 it also gives an
insight into the life of a Victorian family.
**Visiting Times:**
**May - Oct**
Mon - Sat 10a.m. - 5p.m.
Sundays 11a.m. - 5p.m.
Closed for lunch 1pm - 2p.m.		28 **C2**

Tailors' Hall
High Street
Built in 1706 - 1707 this is Dublin's only
surviving guildhall. Restored in recent
times, it now houses An Taisce the Irish
National Trust.
**Visiting Times:**
By appointment only. Phone 4541786
					19 **B3**

Trinity College
College Green
Trinity is a one college university founded
by Queen Elizabeth in 1592. The oldest
buildings now surviving date from 1700.
The multi-media presentation "The Dublin
Experience" in on show from May to
September.
**Visiting Times:**
Mon - Sat 10a.m. - 5p.m.
See also Trinity College Library	20 **D2**

# Parks and Gardens

### Garden of Remembrance
### Parnell Square East, Dublin 1
The Garden of Remembrance was designed by Daithí Hanly and is dedicated to the memory of those who died in the cause of Irish freedom. The garden is open daily during daylight hours.   12 **C3**

### Herbert Park
### Ballsbridge
A charming mature park, well laid out with interesting trees, shrubs and flower beds. An attractive feature is the large pond on the eastern side of the park.        30 **C3**

### Irish National War Memorial Park
### Islandbridge
Designed by the English architect Sir Edward Lutyens, these gardens are dedicated to the memory of 49,400 Irish soldiers who died in the First World War. The Gardens are open every day all year round during daylight hours.      17 **A2**

### Merrion Square Park
### Merrion Square
Formerly only for the use of the residents of Merrion Square, this public park is surrounded on all sides by some of Dublin's finest Georgian architecture.
21 **A3**

### National Botanic Gardens
### Botanic Road, Glasnevin
Covering 19.5 hectares, these beautiful gardens contain a huge assortment of trees, plants and shrubs. Rare blooms and palms are housed in the huge Victorian conservatories.
**Visiting Times:**
Mon - Sat
9a.m. - 6p.m. in summer
10a.m. - 4.30p.m. in winter
Sundays
11a.m. - 6p.m. in summer
11a.m. - 4.30p.m. in winter
Admission Free                    3 **A2**

### Pheonix Park
### North-western edge of city
Acknowledged as one of the largest enclosed urban parks in the world, it covers 1,760 acres, with a circumference of seven miles. Close to the main entrance at Parkgate Street are the Peoples Gardens and the Zoological Gardens (see separate entry). Within the park are the residence of the President of Ireland (Áras an Uachtaráin), the American Ambassador's residence and the Ordnance Survey Office.
**Visiting Times:**
Phoenix Park is open to the public at all times but the Peoples Gardens have their own opening times.
Mon - Fri
8.30a.m. - 9p.m. in Summer
8.30a.m. - 4p.m. in Winter
Sat/Sun
10a.m. - 9p.m in Summer
10.30a.m. - 4p.m in Winter
Admission Free
17 **B1**

Irish National War Memorial Park

### St Anne's Park and Gardens
### Mount Prospect Avenue, Clontarf

In a pleasant setting adjacent to Dollymount Strand, the rose gardens in this park cover over three acres alone. The Park and Gardens are open all year round. Admission free. Entrance Howth Road/All Saints Road.    **8 D2**

### St Stephen's Green

Covering twenty-two acres at the top of Grafton Street, St Stephen's Green is right in the heart of the city. The varied land-scaping of this delightful park includes trees, flower beds, a waterfall and an arti-ficial lake. Several notable monuments and sculptures may also be seen.

**Visiting Hours:**
During daylight hours from 8a.m. to 9p.m. Monday to Saturday and from 10a.m. on Sundays and Bank Holidays.
   **28 C1**

### Zoological Gardens
### Phoenix Park

In these outstanding attractive gardens may be seen a large collection of wild animals and birds from all over the world. Spacious houses and outdoor enclosures add to the total effect. Lion breeding has a long and distinguished history at Dublin Zoo. Two natural lakes house pelicans, flamingoes, ducks and geese.

**Visiting Times:**
Weekdays: 9.30a.m. - 6p.m.
Sundays 10.30a.m. - 6p.m.
Last admission 5p.m. daily    **9 A3**

The Peoples Gardens - Phoenix Park

## Art Galleries

### Hugh Lane Municipal Gallery of Modern Art
### Charlemont House, Parnell Square

The building built between 1762 and 1765 was formerly the residence of Lord Charlemont. The gallery has an interesting collection of works by 19th and 20th century artists. Sir Hugh Lane who was drowned in the sinking of the Lusitania in 1915 contributed the nucleus of this collection of pictures.

**Visiting Times:**
Tues - Fri 9.30a.m. - 6p.m.
Thurs open until 8p.m. (Summer only)
Sat 9.30a.m. - 5p.m.
Sun 11a.m. - 5p.m.
Closed Monday
Admission Free    **12 C3**

### National Gallery
### Merrion Lawn, Merrion Square West

The gallery which contains over 2000 pictures, consisted of only 100 pictures when it was officially opened in 1864. As well as representing all the European schools, there is a comprehensive collection of works by Irish artists.
The Art Reference Library is open from Monday to Friday. There are also free public lectures and conducted hours.

**Visiting Times:**
Mon to Sat 10a.m. - 5.30p.m.
Sun 2p.m. - 5p.m.
Thurs open till 8.15p.m.
Restaurant open during gallery hours.
Free public lectures Sundays 3p.m. and Tuesdays 10.30a.m.
Admission Free    **20 D3**

# Museums

## Dublin Civic Museum
**South William Street**

Occupying the former City Assembly House. It contains a permanent collection of exhibits of antiquarian and historical interest pertaining to Dublin City.

**Visiting Times:**
Tues - Fri: 10a.m. - 5.30p.m.
Saturdays 10a.m. - 5p.m.
Sundays 11a.m. - 2p.m.
Closed Monday and Bank Holidays 20 **C3**

## Genealogical Office and Heraldic Museum
**2 Kildare Street, Dublin 2.**

The oldest office of state in Ireland founded in 1552. See the unique heraldic museum with its colourful display of coats of arms, banners and facility.
Avail of the Consultancy Service on ancestry tracing designed to enable you to undertake on your own the task of uncovering your Irish roots.

**Visiting Hours:**
Mon - Fri: 10a.m. - 12.30p.m.
2.p.m. - 4.30p.m.    20 D3

Genealogical Office

## Irish Jewish Museum
**Walworth Road**

Opened in 1985 by President Herzog of Israel who was educated in Dublin.
Housed in a restored synagogue with documents, photographs and memorabilia showing the history of Irish Jews dating back over 150 years.

**Visiting Times:**
**April to Sept**
Tues/Thurs/Sun 11a.m. - 3.30pm

**Oct to April**
Sunday Only 10.30a.m. - 2.30pm    27 **B2**

## National Museum
**Kildare Street**

The museum houses one of the most impressive collection of antiques in Europe. Items displayed cover every age from the Stone Age to Medieval Times. Items of particular interest are the Tara Brooch, the Cross of Cong and the Ardagh Chalice. One of its most recent additions is the Derrynaflan Hoard which was found in a bog in Tipperary in 1980. The main entrance is from Kildare Street but part of the natural history division is approached from Merrion Street.

**Visiting Times:**
Tues - Sat: 10a.m. - 5.30p.m.
Sundays 2p.m. - 5p.m.
Closed Mondays    20 **D3**

## National Wax Museum
**Granby Row**

On display are life-size figures of prominent Irish historical, political, theatrical, literary and sporting personalities. Taped narrations on each scene, guide one along.

**Visiting Times:**
Mon - Sat: 10a.m. - 5.30p.m.
Sundays 12 noon - 5.30p.m.    11 **B3**

## The Writer's Museum
**18/19 Parnell Square North**

Opened in 1991 in two restored Georgian houses. It features a display of paintings, photographs, manuscripts and other memorabilia relating to Irish writers such as Shaw, Yeats, Beckett, Wilde, O'Casey, Joyce, Behan and Swift.

**Visiting Times:**
Mon - Sat: 10a.m. - 5.30p.m.
Sundays and Bank Holidays
11a.m. - 5p.m.    20 **C3**

## Phoenix Park Visitor Centre
### Phoenix Park

Located 5kms from the City Centre. The Tower House close to the visitor centre possibly dates from the 17th Century.
There are exhibitions, a film show and visitors can view a colourful and realistic interpretation of the past.

**Visiting Times:**
**Nov - Mid March**
9.30a.m. - 4.30p.m. Sat/Sun
**Mid March - Late March**
9.30a.m. - 5p.m. Daily
**April - May**
9.30a.m. -5.30p.m. Daily
**June - Sept**
10a.m. - 6p.m. Daily
**Oct** 9.30a.m. - 5p.m. Daily
Last admission 45 minutes before closing. Free guided tours of Áras an Uachtaráin Saturdays only. Phone 6709155     9 **A3**

## Dublinia - Christ Church
### St Michael's Hill

The realistic and novel exhibition that is Dublinia is situated in the old Synod Hall on St Michael's Hill, alongside of Christ Church Cathedral, to which it is connected by an ornate pedistrian archway over St Michael's Hill.
The exhibition heralds the arrival of the Anglo-Normans in 1170 through a broad spectrum of Dublin life to the closure of the Monasteries in 1540.

**Visiting Times:**
**Summer**
10a.m. - 5p.m. Daily
**Winter** (Oct 1st - March 31st)
Mon - Sat 11a.m. - 4p.m.
Sun 10a.m. - 4.30p.m.     19 **B3**

## Dunsink Observatory
### Dunsink Lane, near Castleknock

Founded in 1783, this is one of the world's oldest observatories. It formerly belonged to Trinity College but is now the centre of the School of Astronomical Physics of the Dublin Institute for Advanced Studies.

**Visiting Times:**
Open to the public on the first and third Wednesday of each month from October to March, at 8p.m. Admission free on written application to the secretary enclosing stamp-addressed envelope. 9 **A1**

## The James Joyce Centre
### 35 North Great Georges Street

The centre is housed in a beautifully restored 18th century Georgian Town-house only 300 metres from O'Connell Street. The aim of the centre is to promote an interest in the life and works of James Joyce and to this end there are daily talks, conducted tours of the house and walks through the heartland of Joyce's North inner city.

**Visiting Times:**
Mon - Sat 9.30a.m. - 5p.m.
Sunday 12.30p.m. - 5p.m.     12 **C3**

## Waterways Visitor Centre
### Grand Canal Quay, Dublin 2

The centre houses an exhibition outlining the history of Ireland's inland waterways and the activities and experiences current-ly available.
Featuring an audio-visual show and work-ing models of various engineering fea-tures.

**Visiting Times:**
**June - September**
9.30a.m. - 6.30p.m. daily
**Oct - May**
Wed to Sun 12.30p.m. - 5p.m.
Last admission 45 minutes before closing.
21 **B3**

Waterways Visitor Centre

# Churches and Cathedrals

### Christ Church Cathedral
### Christchurch Place
Built in 1173 by Strongbow on a site originally occupied by a church built in 1030 by Sitric the Viking King. The present structure dates from the 19th century, although the medieval crypt still remains. It contains many interesting historical remains.
**Visiting Times:**
10 a.m. - 5.30 p.m. All year
Group tours available on request/ application                                    **19 B3**

### St Anne's Church
### Dawson Street
Designed by Isaac Wells in neoromanesque style in 1720. The facade was added by Sir Thomas Deane in 1868.
                                                           **20 D3**

### St Audoen's Church
### High Street.
St Audoen's dates from medieval times and is the oldest of Dublin's parish churches. The tower houses Ireland's three most ancient bells, dating from 1423. St Audoen's Arch stands nearby. This is Dublin's only surviving city gate. St Audoen's Heritage Centre is due to open in Summer 1999.
**Visiting Times:**
To be decided
Phone 6613105 for further information
                                                           **19 A3**

### St Mary's Abbey
### Meetinghouse Lane (off Capel St.)
The Abbey was founded in 1139 as a daughter house of the Benedictine Order of Savigny. It was one of the largest and most important monasteries in Ireland. The Chapter House is all that remains of the Abbey which houses an interesting historical exhibition.
**Visiting Times:**
**Mid June - Mid Sept.**
Wed and Sun only 10a.m. - 5p.m.
Last tour 45 minutes before closing.
                                                           **19 B2**

### St Mary's Church
### Mary Street
Dating from 1627, this was the first Dublin church to be built with galleries. Theobald Wolfe Tone was baptised here in 1763 and Sean O'Casey the playwright in 1880. This church is now a retail outlet    **19 B1**

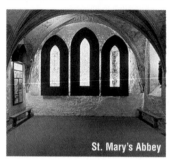
St. Mary's Abbey

### St Mary's Pro-Cathedral
### Marlborough Street
Designed by John Sweetman and built between 1815 and 1825 in the Great Down Style. The Metropolitan Church of the diocese, it is used for state functions.
                                                           **20 C1**

### St Michan's Church
### Church Street
Founded by the Norse in 1096, the present building dates from 1685-6, having been much restored in 1828. The church's Harris organ is said to have been used by Handel during his visit to Dublin.
Vaults beneath the church contain mummified corpses which may be seen by the public.
**Visiting Times:**
Church and Vaults:
**April - Oct.**
Mon - Fri 10a.m. - 5p.m.
**Nov - March**
Mon - Fri 12.30p.m. - 3.30p.m.
Saturday 10a.m. - 1p.m.
Vaults closed on Sunday          **19 A2**

## St Patrick's Cathedral
### Patrick Street

Built on the site of a 6th century church said to have been founded by St Patrick himself. The present church was commenced in 1191. In 1213 it gained Cathedral status. A university was established there in 1320 but was suppressed by Henry VIII. The square tower was built in the 14th century and houses the largest ringing bells in Ireland. Jonathan Swift was Dean of St Patrick's from 1713 to 1745.

**Visiting Times:**
Mon - Fri 9a.m. - 6p.m.
Saturday 9a.m. - 5p.m.
Sunday **April - Sept** 9.30a.m. - 5p.m.
**Oct - March** 10a.m. - 5p.m.
Except during Sunday Service
11a.m. - 12.45p.m. and 3p.m. - 4.15p.m.
Closed 4p.m. Nov - March          19 **B3**

## St Werburgh's Cathedral
### Werburgh Street

Erected in 1715 on the site of the medieval successor to pre Norman St Werburgh's. Destroyed by fire in 1754, the church was re-opened in 1759. In the vaults beneath the church is buried Lord Edward Fitzgerald.

**Visiting Times:**
By appointment only.
Tel: 4783710
Mon - Fri 10a.m. - 4p.m.          19 **B3**
Service 10a.m.

## University Church
### St Stephen's Green

Founded by Cardinal Newman, it was designed in a neo-Byzantine style by John Hungerford Pollen. It was built between 1854 and 1856.

28 **C1**

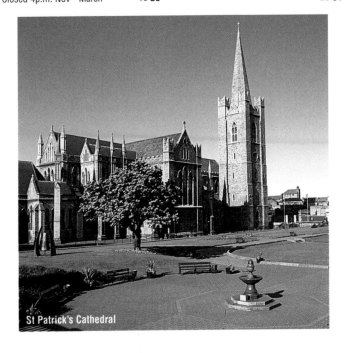
St Patrick's Cathedral

# Libraries

## Chester Beatty Library
### Dublin Castle
On of the world's most valuable private collections of oriental manuscripts and miniatures can be seen here. There are manuscripts of the New Testament, Manichean papyri and Eastern miniatures, as well as picture scrolls, albums and jades from the Far East. The library is located in the Clock Tower building and will open daily from Spring 2000.

19 **B3**

## Marsh's Library
### St Patrick's Close
This is Ireland's oldest public library, founded in 1701 by Archbishop Narcissus Marsh. The collection consists mainly of theological, medical, ancient historical, Hebrew, Syriac, Greek, French and Latin literature.
**Visiting Hours:**
Weekdays 10a.m. - 12.45p.m.
          2p.m. - 5p.m.
Saturday 10.30a.m. - 12.45p.m.
Closed Tuesdays, Sundays and Bank Holidays

27 **B1**

## National Library
### Kildare Street
Founded in 1877 this is Ireland's largest public library. It contains over half a million books as well as maps, prints and manuscripts. It also houses a large newspaper collection.
**Visiting Times:**
Mon - Wed (incl) 10a.m. - 9p.m.
Thurs/Fri 10a.m. - 5p.m.
Saturday 10a.m. to 1p.m.

20 **D3**

## Royal Irish Academy Library
### 19 Dawson Street
One of the most extensive collections of ancient Irish manuscripts can be seen here. These include the *Book of the Dun Cow* the *Book of Ballymote*, the *Speckled Book*, the *Slowe Missal* and the *Cathac* or *Battle Book* reputed to be the actual copy of the Psalms made in the 6th century by St Colmcille.
**Visiting Times:**
Mon - Fri 10.30a.m. - 5p.m.
Closed Bank Holidays and during the last three weeks of August.
Admission Free

20 **D3**

Trinity College - Entrance

## Trinity College Library
### College Green
Dating from the late sixteenth century, Trinity College Library is Ireland's oldest library. It contains over 1,000,000 volumes and Ireland's most extensive collection of manuscripts and early printed books. Its greatest treasure is the Book of Kells (probably eight century).
The library is housed in two buildings - the Old Library (completed in 1732) and the New Library (1967).
**Visiting Times:**
Mon - Sat 9.30a.m. to 5p.m.
**October - May**
Sunday 12 noon to 4.30p.m.
**June -September**
Sun. 9.30a.m. to 4.30p.m.

20 **D2**

| Street Name | Page/Grid Ref. |
|---|---|
| 1 Branch Rd N | 23 A1 |
| 1 Branch Rd S | 23 A1 |
| 2 Branch Rd N | 23 B1 |
| 2 Branch Rd S | 23 A1 |
| 3 Branch Rd S | 23 A1 |
| 4 Branch Rd S | 23 B1 |
| Abbey Cottages | 20 C2[2] |
| Abbey Court | 7 B1 |
| Abbey Park | 7 B1 |
| Abbey Street Lr | 20 D1 |
| Abbey Street Mid | 20 C2 |
| Abbey Street Old | 20 D1 |
| Abbey Street Upr | 19 B2 |
| Abbeyfield | 8 C1 |
| Abercorn Road | 21 B1 |
| Aberdeen Street | 18 C1 |
| Achill Road | 4 D2 |
| Adair | 30 D3[4] |
| Adair Lane | 20 C2[3] |
| Addison Place | 3 B2 |
| Addison Road | 13 B1 |
| Adelaide Court | 28 C2 |
| Adelaide Road | 28 C2 |
| Adelaide Terrace | 25 B1 |
| Aikenhead Terrace | 22 D3 |
| Albert Court | 21 B3 |
| Albert Place East | 21 B3[8] |
| Albert Place West | 28 C2 |
| Albert Terrace | 28 C2[11] |
| Aldborough Parade | 13 A3 |
| Aldborough Place | 13 A3 |
| Aldborough Square | 13 A3[12] |
| Alexandra Quay | 22 D2[2] |
| Alexandra Quay | 23 A1 |
| (Apts) | |
| Alexandra Road | 23 A1 |
| Alexandra Rd Ext | 24 D1 |
| Alexandra Terrace | 22 C1 |
| (North Wall) | |
| Alexandra Terrace | 27 B2 |
| Alfie Byrne Road | 14 C2 |
| Allingham Street | 26 D1 |
| Almeida Avenue | 17 B3[8] |
| Almeida Terrace | 25 B1[1] |
| Alverno | 15 B2[1] |
| Amiens Street | 13 A3 |
| Anglesea Road | 30 C3 |
| Anglesea Row | 19 B1 |
| Anglesea Street | 20 C2 |
| Annadale Avenue | 5 B3 |
| Annadale Crescent | 5 B2 |
| Annadale Drive | 5 B2 |
| Annaly Road | 10 D1 |

| Street Name | Page/Grid Ref. |
|---|---|
| Annamoe Drive | 10 D2 |
| Annamoe Parade | 10 D2 |
| Annamoe Park | 10 D2 |
| Annamoe Road | 10 C2 |
| Annamoe Terrace | 10 D2 |
| Anne Street North | 19 B1 |
| Anne Street South | 20 C3 |
| Anne's Lane | 20 C3 |
| Anner Road | 25 A1 |
| Annesley Avenue | 13 B2[2] |
| Annesley Bridge Rd | 13 B2 |
| Annesley Place | 13 B2 |
| Aranmore Avenue | 11 B2[7] |
| Arbour Hill | 18 C1 |
| Arbour Place | 18 D1 |
| Arbour Terrace | 18 C1 |
| Arbutus Avenue | 27 A3 |
| Arbutus Place | 27 B2 |
| Ard Righ Place | 18 D1 |
| Ard Righ Road | 18 D1 |
| Ardagh Road | 25 B3 |
| Ardee Grove | 27 B3 |
| Ardee Road | 28 C3 |
| Ardee Row | 27 A1 |
| Ardee Street | 27 A1 |
| Ardilaun Road | 13 A2 |
| Ardmore Avenue | 10 C2 |
| Ardoyne House | 29 B3[3] |
| Ardpatrick Road | 9 A1 |
| Argyle Road | 29 B3 |
| Arklow Street | 10 C3 |
| Armstrong Street | 27 A3[3] |
| Army Road | 17 A1 |
| Arnott Street | 27 B1 |
| Arran Quay | 19 A2 |
| Arran Quay Terrace | 19 A2 |
| Arran Road | 4 D2 |
| Arran Street East | 19 B2 |
| Arran Street West | 19 A2 |
| Asdill's Row | 20 C2[5] |
| Ash Grove | 19 A3[14] |
| Ash Street | 19 A3 |
| Ashbrook | 7 A3 |
| Ashford Cottages | 10 C3[2] |
| Ashford Place | 10 C3[1] |
| Ashford Street | 10 C3 |
| Ashington Court | 1 A2 |
| Ashington Mews | 1 A2 |
| Ashling Close | 25 B3 |
| Ashmount Court | 17 A3[8] |
| Ashworth Place | 27 B3[3] |
| Aston Place | 20 C2 |
| Aston Quay | 20 C2 |

| Street Name | Page/Grid Ref. |
|---|---|
| Athlumney Villas | 28 C3 |
| Auburn Street | 11 B3 |
| Auburn Terrace | 17 B3[10] |
| Auburn Walk | 10 C3 |
| Aughavanagh Rd | 26 D3 |
| Aughrim Court | 10 D3[4] |
| Aughrim Lane | 10 D3 |
| Aughrim Place | 10 C3 |
| Aughrim Street | 10 C3 |
| Aughrim Villas | 10 D3[1] |
| Aungier Lane | 28 C1[1] |
| Aungier Place | 28 C1 |
| Aungier Street | 20 C3 |
| Austin's Cottages | 13 B2[10] |
| Ave Maria Road | 26 C1 |
| Avenue Road | 27 B2 |
| Avondale Avenue | 11 A2 |
| Avondale House | 12 D3[19] |
| Avondale Road | 11 A2 |
| Bachelor's Walk | 20 C2 |
| Bachelor's Way | 20 C2 |
| Back Lane | 19 B3 |
| Baggot Court | 29 A1 |
| Baggot Street Lwr | 29 A1 |
| Baggot Street Upr | 29 A2 |
| Baggotrath Place | 29 A1[2] |
| Bailey's Row | 13 A3 |
| Balfe Street | 20 C3[3] |
| Ball's Lane | 19 B1 |
| Ballsbridge | 30 C3 |
| Ballsbridge Avenue | 30 C3 |
| Ballsbridge Gardens | 30 C2 |
| Ballsbridge Park | 30 D3[6] |
| Ballsbridge Terrace | 30 C3[1] |
| Ballsbridge Wood | 30 C2 |
| Ballyboggan Road | 1 A1 |
| Ballybough Avenue | 13 A2[15] |
| Ballybough Court | 13 A2[14] |
| Ballybough Lane | 13 A2[12] |
| Ballybough Road | 13 A2 |
| Ballygall Road East | 3 A1 |
| Ballymun Road | 3 B1 |
| Bangor Drive | 25 B3 |
| Bangor Road | 25 B3 |
| Bann Road | 2 C2 |
| Bannaville | 28 C3[4] |
| Bannow Road | 1 B2 |
| Bantry Road | 4 C1 |
| Bargy Road | 14 C3 |
| Barnamore Grove | 1 A1 |
| Barnamore Park | 1 A1 |
| Barrack Lane | 30 D1[3] |
| Barrow Place | 4 C2 |

Barrow Road 2 C2
Barrow Street 22 C3
Basin Street Lwr 18 C3
Basin Street Upr 18 C3
Bass Place 21 A3
Bath Avenue 30 C1
Bath Ave Gdns 30 C1
Bath Avenue Place 30 C1
Bath Lane 12 C3
Bath Street 22 D3
Bayview Avenue 13 A2
Beach Avenue 31 A1
Beach Drive 31 A1
Beach Road 31 A1
Beatty's Avenue 30 C2
Beaucourt 4 D2[1]
Beaver Close 13 A3[9]
Beaver Street 13 A3
Bective Square 11 B2[11]
Bedford Lane 20 C2
Bedford Row 20 C2[4]
Beggars Bush Court 30 C1[6]
Belgrove Road 16 D1
Bell's Lane 28 D1
Bella Avenue 12 D3[7]
Bella Place 12 D3[6]
Bella Street 12 D3
Bellevue 18 D3
Bellevue Cottages 2 D1[1]
Bellman's Walk 21 B1
Belmont Place 12 D3[16]
Belton Park Avenue 6 D1
Belton Park Gardens 6 D1
Belton Park Road 6 D1
Belton Park Villas 6 D2
Belvidere Avenue 12 D2[5]
Belvidere Court 12 C2
Belvidere Place 12 D2
Belvidere Road 12 C2
Ben Edar Road 10 C3
Benbulbin Avenue 25 A2
Benbulbin Rd 25 A2
Benburb Street 18 D2
Bengal Terrace 3 A3
Benson Street 22 C2
Beresford Avenue 5 A2
Beresford Green 5 A2
Beresford Lawn 5 A2
Beresford Place 20 D1
Beresford Street 19 B1
Berkeley Avenue 11 B2
Berkeley Mews 30 C1[5]
Berkeley Place 11 B2
Berkeley Road 11 B2
Berkeley Street 11 B2

Berkeley Terrace 30 C1
Berystede 29 A3[2]
Bessborough Ave 13 B2
Bessborough Pde 28 C3
Bethany House 31 B3[1]
Bethesda Place 12 C3[8]
Beverly Court 8 D3
Bishop Street 27 B1
Black Street 17 B1[2]
Blackberry Lane 28 C3
Blackhall Parade 19 A1
Blackhall Place 18 D2
Blackhall Street 19 A1
Blackheath Avenue 8 C3
Blackheath Court 8 D3
Blackheath Drive 8 C3
Blackheath Gardens 8 C3
Blackheath Grove 8 C3
Blackheath Park 8 C3
Blackhorse Avenue 9 A2
Blackhorse Grove 10 C3
Blackpitts 27 A1
Blackwater Road 2 C2
Blessington Court 11 B3[7]
Blessington Lane 11 B3
Blessington Place 11 B2[13]
Blessington Street 11 B3
Bloomfield Avenue 27 B2
Bloomfield Avenue 29 A3
 (Ranelagh)
Bloomfield Cottages 27 B2[6]
Bloomfield Park 27 B2
Blythe Avenue 21 B1[2]
Boardman's Lane 26 C1[5]
Bond Drive 15 A3
Bond Road 14 D3
Bond Street 18 D3
Bonham Street 18 D2
Boolavogue Road 14 C3[1]
Borris Court 19 B3[5]
Botanic Avenue 4 C3
Botanic Park 4 C3
Botanic Road 3 B3
Botanic Villas 3 B3
Boundary Road 14 D2
Bow Bridge 18 C3
Bow Lane East 20 C3
Bow Lane West 18 C3
Bow Street 19 A1
Boyne Lane 21 A3
Boyne Road 1 B2
Boyne Street 21 A3
Brabazon Place 27 A1[8]
Brabazon Row 27 A1
Brabazon Square 19 A3[1]

Brabazon Street 19 A3[7]
Bracken's Lane 20 D2[3]
Brainsboro Terrace 27 A2[4]
Braithwaite Street 18 D3
Brandon Terrace 26 D1[4]
Breakwater Rd Nth 24 C1
Breakwater Rd Sth 24 C1
Bregia Road 10 D1
Bremen Avenue 23 A3
Bremen Grove 23 A3
Bremen Road 23 A3
Brenden Behan Ct 12 D2[16]
Brian Avenue 6 C3
Brian Boru Avenue 16 D2
Brian Boru Street 16 D2
Brian Road 6 C3/13 B1
Brian Terrace 13 B1
Brickfield Drive 25 B2
Brickfield Lane 26 D1
Bride Close 19 B2[17]
Bride Court 19 B3[17]
Bride Road 19 B3
Bride Street 19 B3
Bridge Court 29 B1[8]
Bridge Street 22 D3
Bridge Street Lower 19 A2
Bridge Street Upper 19 A2
Bridgefoot Street 19 A2
Bridgewater Quay 17 A2
Brighton Avenue 6 D3
Britain Place 12 C3[10]
Britain Quay 22 C2
Broadstone Avenue 11 B3[12]
Brodin Row 18 C1
Brookfield Road 17 B3
Brookfield Street 25 B1
Brooklawn 15 A1
Brookwood Ave 8 D1
Brookwood Glen 8 D1
Brookwood Meadow 8 C1
Brookwood Park 8 C1
Brookwood Rise 8 D1
Broombridge Road 1 B2
Brown Street North 19 A1
Brown Street South 26 D1
Brunswick Place 21 B3
Brunswick St Nth 19 A1
Brunswick Villas 20 D2[4]
Buckingham Place 13 A3[6]
Buckingham St Lwr 13 A3
Buckingham St Upr 13 A3
Buckingham Village 12 D3[12]
Bulfin Gardens 17 A3
Bulfin Road 25 A1
Bull Alley Street 19 B3

| | | |
|---|---|---|
| Burgess Lane | 19 A2[1] | |
| Burgh Quay | 20 D2 | |
| Burke Place | 18 C3 | |
| Burleigh Court | 29 A2 | |
| Burlington Gardens | 29 A2 | |
| Burlington Road | 29 A2 | |
| Byrne's Lane | 20 C2 | |
| Cabra | 10 C1 | |
| Cabra Drive | 10 C2 | |
| Cabra Grove | 10 C2 | |
| Cabra Park | 11 A1 | |
| Cabra Road | 10 C2 | |
| Cadogan Road | 13 B1 | |
| Calderwood Avenue | 5 B1 | |
| Calderwood Grove | 5 B2 | |
| Calderwood Road | 5 B1 | |
| Caledon Road | 14 C3 | |
| Camac Terrace | 17 B3[16] | |
| Cambridge Avenue | 23 A3 | |
| Cambridge Court | 22 D3[1] | |
| Cambridge Road | 22 D3 | |
| Cambridge Square | 22 D2[3] | |
| Cambridge Street | 22 D2 | |
| Cambridge Terrace | 28 D3 | |
| Camden Buildings | 28 C1[6] | |
| Camden Court | 28 C2[1] | |
| Camden Lock | 22 C3 | |
| Camden Market | 28 C2[3] | |
| Camden Place | 28 C1 | |
| Camden Row | 27 B1 | |
| Camden St Lwr | 28 C1 | |
| Camden St Old | 28 C2[2] | |
| Camden St Upr | 28 C2 | |
| Camden Villas | 28 C1[5] | |
| Cameron Square | 17 B3 | |
| Cameron Street | 26 D1 | |
| Camogie Road | 17 A1 | |
| Campbell's Court | 19 B1 | |
| Campbell's Lane | 12 D2[6] | |
| Campbell's Row | 12 D2[7] | |
| Canal Road | 28 C3 | |
| Canon Lillis Avenue | 13 B3 | |
| Canon Mews East | 30 C1[9] | |
| Canon Mooney Gdns | 22 D3[2] | |
| Caragh Court | 13 B1[1] | |
| Caragh Road | 9 B2 | |
| Carberry Road | 5 B1 | |
| Carbury Terrace | 22 C1[1] | |
| Cardiff Lane | 21 B2 | |
| Cards Lane | 20 D2[5] | |
| Carleton Road | 6 C3 | |
| Carlingford Parade | 21 B2 | |
| Carlingford Road | 4 C3 | |
| Carlisle Street | 27 B2 | |
| Carlton Court | 15 A1 | |
| Carlton Villas | 30 C2[3] | |
| Carman's Hall | 19 A3 | |
| Carnew Street | 10 C3 | |
| Carnlough Road | 1 B3/10 C1 | |
| Caroline Row | 22 D3 | |
| Carrick Terrace | 26 C1 | |
| Carrickfoyle Tce | 17 A3[5] | |
| Carrigallen Drive | 1 B1 | |
| Carrigallen Park | 1 B1 | |
| Carrigallen Road | 1 B1 | |
| Casino Park | 6 D2 | |
| Casino Road | 5 B3 | |
| Castilla Park | 8 D3 | |
| Castle Avenue | 8 C3/15 B1 | |
| Castle Court | 7 A3 | |
| Castle Grove | 7 B3 | |
| Castle Market | 20 C3 | |
| Castle Road | 16 C1 | |
| Castle Street | 19 B3 | |
| Castle Terrace | 11 A2[1] | |
| Castleforbes Road | 22 C1 | |
| Cathal Brugha St | 20 C1 | |
| Cathedral Lane | 27 B1 | |
| Cathedral Street | 20 C1 | |
| Cathedral View Ct | 27 B1 | |
| Cathedral View Wk | 27 B1[5] | |
| Catherine Court | 13 A3 | |
| Catherine Lane N | 19 A1[3] | |
| Catherine Street | 19 A3 | |
| Cavendish Row | 12 C3[9] | |
| Ceannt Fort | 17 B3[9] | |
| Cecil Avenue | 6 D3 | |
| Cecilia Street | 20 C2[8] | |
| Celestine Avenue | 22 D3 | |
| Celtic Park Avenue | 6 D1 | |
| Celtic Park Road | 6 C1 | |
| Chamber Street | 27 A1 | |
| Champion's Avenue | 20 D1 | |
| Champion Quay | 20 C2[11] | |
| Chancery Lane | 19 B3 | |
| Chancery Place | 19 B2 | |
| Chancery Street | 19 B2 | |
| Chapel Avenue | 22 D3 | |
| Chapel Lane | 19 B1 | |
| Charlemont | 6 C1 | |
| Charlemont Grdns | 28 C2[7] | |
| Charlemont Mall | 28 C2 | |
| Charlemont Parade | 13 A2[8] | |
| Charlemont Place | 28 C2[14] | |
| Charlemont Place | 28 D2 | |
| Charlemont Road | 6 D3 | |
| Charlemont Street | 28 C2 | |
| Charles Lane | 12 D2 | |
| Charles St Gt | 12 D3 | |
| Charles St W | 19 B2 | |
| Charleville Avenue | 13 A2 | |
| Charleville Mall | 13 A2 | |
| Charleville Road | 10 D2 | |
| Charlotte Quay | 22 C3 | |
| Charlotte Way | 28 C2 | |
| Chatham Court | 20 C3[14] | |
| Chatham Lane | 20 C2[5] | |
| Chatham Row | 20 C3[5] | |
| Chatham Street | 20 C3 | |
| Chelmsford Avenue | 28 D3 | |
| Chelmsford Road | 29 A3 | |
| Chelsea Gardens | 16 D1 | |
| Cheltenham Place | 28 C3[3] | |
| Cherrymount Cres | 6 D2[3] | |
| Cherrymount Grove | 6 D2[2] | |
| Cherrymount Park | 11 A2 | |
| Chesterfield Avenue | 17 A1 | |
| Christchurch Place | 19 B3 | |
| Christchurch Sq | 19 B3[9] | |
| Church Avenue | 3 B1 | |
| Church Avenue (Drumcondra) | 4 D2 | |
| Church Avenue (East Wall) | 22 C1[4] | |
| Church Avenue (Irishtown) | 30 D1 | |
| Church Ave S | 26 C1 | |
| Church Ave W | 19 A1 | |
| Church Lane | 20 C2 | |
| Church Lane South | 27 B1[6] | |
| Church Place | 22 C1[3] | |
| Church Road | 13 B3 | |
| Church Road | 14 C3 | |
| Church Row | 22 C1[5] | |
| Church Street | 19 A2 | |
| Church St East | 22 C1 | |
| Church St New | 19 A2 | |
| Church St Upr | 19 A1 | |
| Church Terrace | 19 A1 | |
| Churchgate Avenue | 16 D2[1] | |
| Churchill Terrace | 30 D3[5] | |
| Cian Park | 4 D3 | |
| City Quay | 21 A2 | |
| Clanawley Road | 7 B2 | |
| Clanboy Road | 7 B1 | |
| Clanbrassil Close | 27 A2 | |
| Clanbrassil St Lwr | 27 A2 | |
| Clanbrassil St Upr | 27 A2 | |
| Clancarthy Road | 7 A2 | |
| Clandonagh Road | 7 A1 | |
| Clanhugh Road | 7 B2 | |
| Clanmahon Road | 7 B1 | |
| Clanmaurice Road | 7 A1 | |
| Clanmoyle Road | 7 A2 | |
| Clanranald Road | 7 A1 | |

Clanree Road 7 A1
Clanwilliam Court 29 B1[6]
Clanwilliam Place 29 B1
Clanwilliam Square 21 B3[5]
Clanwilliam Terrace 21 B3[6]
Clare Lane 20 D3
Clare Park Villas 4 D1
Clare Road 4 D1
Clare Street 20 D3
Claremont Avenue 3 B1
Claremont Close 31 A2[5]
Claremont Close 2 D3
Claremont Court 2 D2
   (Glasnevin)
Claremont Court 30 D2[4]
   (Sandymount)
Claremont Crescent 2 D2
Claremont Lawns 3 A3
Claremont Park 31 A2
Claremont Road 31 A2
Clarence Mangan Rd 27 A1
Clarence Mangan Sq 19 B3[16]
Clarence Pl Gt 21 B3
Clarence St Gt N 13 A3
Clarendon Market 20 C3[6]
Clarendon Row 20 C3[13]
Clarendon Street 20 C3
Clareville Court 3 A3
Clareville Grove 3 A3
Clarke's Terrace 26 C1
Claude Road 11 B1
Cliftonville Road 3 B3
Clinch's Court 13 A2[6]
Clogher Road 26 C3
Cloister Court 1 A2[1]
Clonard Road 25 A3
Clonlara Road 23 A3
Clonliffe Avenue 13 A2
Clonliffe Gardens 13 A1
Clonliffe Road 12 D1/13 A1
Clonmel Street 28 C1
Clonmore Court 3 B1
Clonmore Road 13 A2
Clonmore Terrace 13 A2
Clonmore Villas 13 A2[4]
Clontarf Park 16 D2
Clontarf Road 14 D1/16 D2
Clonturk Avenue 4 D2
Clonturk Gardens 4 D3[2]
Clonturk Park 4 D3
Cloonlara Crescent 1 B1
Clyde Lane 29 B3
Clyde Road 29 B3
Coburg Street 13 A3
Coke Lane 19 A2[2]

Coke Ovens Cotts 2 D3[1]
Colbert's Fort 26 C1[2]
Coleraine Street 19 B1
College Green 20 C2
College Lane 21 A3[4]
College Street 20 D2
Collins Avenue 6 C1
Collins Avenue East 7 A2
Collins Court 6 C1
Collins Park 6 D1
Commons Street 21 A1
Comyn Place 4 C2
Con Colbert Road 17 A3
Connaught Parade 11 A1[1]
Connaught Street 11 A1
Conquer Hill Ave 16 D2
Constitution Hill 11 B3
Constitution Hill (Flats) 19 B1[3]
Convent Avenue 13 A1
Convent Close 29 A1[1]
Convent Place 28 D2[1]
Convent View Cotts 1 A3
Convent View Cres 1 A3
Conway Court 21 B3[9]
Conyngham Road 17 B2
Cook Street 19 A2
Coolevin Road 27 B1
Coombe Court 19 A3[8]
Cope Street 20 C2
Copeland Avenue 6 D3
Copeland Grove 6 D3
Copper Alley 19 B2
Coppinger Row 20 C3[4]
Cork Hill 19 B2[8]
Cork Street 26 D1
Corn Exchange Pl 20 D2[1]
Cornmarket 19 A3
Corporation Street 20 D1
Countess Markievicz 21 A2[5]
   House
Courtney Place 13 B2[1]
Cow Parlour 27 A1[4]
Cowper Street 10 C3
Craigford Avenue 7 B1
Craigford Drive 7 B1
Crampton Court 20 C2[9]
Crane Lane 19 B2
Crane Street 18 D3
Cranfield Place 31 A1
Cranmer Lane 29 B1[1]
Crawford Avenue 4 C3
Creighton Street 21 A2
Cremore Avenue 3 A1
Cremore Crescent 3 A1
Cremore Drive 3 A1

Cremore Lawn 2 D1
Cremore Park 3 A1
Cremore Road 3 A1
Cremore Villas 3 A1
Crescent Gardens 13 B2
Crescent House 14 D1[1]
Crescent Place 13 B2
Crescent Villas 4 C3
Crinan Strand 21 A1
Croagh Patrick Rd 9 A1
Cromwell's Quarters 18 C3
Crosbie House 28 D3[5]
Cross Kevin Street 27 B1[8]
Crostick Alley 19 A3[15]
Crow Street 20 C2
Crown Alley 20 C2
Croydon Gardens 5 B3
Croydon Green 5 B3
Croydon Pk Ave 6 C3
Croydon Terrace 5 B3
Crumlin Road 25 A3
Cuala Road 10 D1
Cuckoo Lane 19 B1
Cuffe Lane 28 C1
Cuffe Street 28 C1
Cullen's Wood 28 D3[7]
Cumberland Court 21 A3[3]
Cumberland Road 29 A2
Cumberland St Nth 12 D3
Cumberland St Sth 21 A3
Curved Street 20 C2[14]
Curzon Street 27 B2
Custom Hall 20 D1[9]
Custom Ho. Quay 20 D1
Cymbric Road 23 A3
Dalcassian Downs 11 A1
Dalymount 11 A2
Dame Court 20 C2
Dame Lane 20 C2
Dame Street 20 C2
Danesfort 15 B2
Daneswell Road 3 B3
Daniel Street 27 B1
Dargle Road 4 C3
Darley Street 27 A3
Darley's Terrace 26 D1
Dartmouth Lane 28 D3
Dartmouth Place 28 D3
Dartmouth Road 28 D3
Dartmouth Sq E 28 D3
Dartmouth Sq N 28 D2
Dartmouth Sq Sth 28 D3
Dartmouth Sq W 28 D3
Dartmouth Terrace 28 D3
David Park 11 B1

| | | |
|---|---|---|
| David Road | 11 B1 | |
| Davis Place | 19 B3[2] | |
| Davitt Road | 25 A1 | |
| Dawson Lane | 20 D3 | |
| Dawson Street | 20 D3 | |
| De Burgh Road | 18 C2[1] | |
| De Courcy Square | 3 B3 | |
| De Valera Place | 12 C2[9] | |
| Dean Street | 27 B1 | |
| Dean Swift Square | 19 A3 | |
| Delvin Road | 10 D1 | |
| Delvin Terrace | 11 B3[16] | |
| Demesne | 8 C2 | |
| Denmark St Great | 12 C3 | |
| Denzille Lane | 21 A3 | |
| Dermot O'Hurley Ave | 22 D3 | |
| Derrynane Gardens | 22 D3 | |
| Derrynane Parade | 12 C2[3] | |
| Desmond Street | 27 B2 | |
| Deverell Place | 20 D1[6] | |
| Devery's Lane | 11 B1 | |
| Devlin's Place | 21 A3 | |
| Devoy Road | 25 A1 | |
| Dexter Terrace | 28 D3[1] | |
| Digges Lane | 20 C3 | |
| Digges St Upr | 28 C1 | |
| Dillon Place South | 19 B3 | |
| Dingle Road | 9 B1 | |
| Distillery Road | 13 A1 | |
| Dodder Terrace | 22 D3 | |
| Dodder View Cotts | 30 C2[5] | |
| D'Olier Street | 20 D2 | |
| Dolphin Avenue | 26 D2 | |
| Dolphin House | 26 D2 | |
| Dolphin Park | 25 B2 | |
| Dolphin Road | 25 B2 | |
| Dolphin's Barn | 26 C2 | |
| Dolphin's Barn St | 26 C2 | |
| Dominick Lane | 19 B1 | |
| Dominick Place | 20 C1 | |
| Dominick St Lwr | 19 B1 | |
| Dominick St Upr | 11 B3 | |
| Donelan Avenue | 18 C3 | |
| Donnycarney | 6 D1 | |
| Donnycarney Road | 6 D2 | |
| Donore Avenue | 26 D1 | |
| Donore Road | 26 D1 | |
| Donore Terrace | 26 D1 | |
| Donovan Lane | 27 A2 | |
| Doon Avenue | 10 C2 | |
| Doris Street | 22 C3 | |
| Dorset Lane | 12 C2 | |
| Dorset Place | 12 C2 | |
| Dorset Street Lwr | 12 C2 | |
| Dorset Street Upr | 11 B3 | |
| Dowling's Court | 21 A2 | |
| Downpatrick Road | 25 B3 | |
| Dowth Avenue | 10 D1 | |
| Dromard Terrace | 31 A1 | |
| Drumalee Avenue | 10 C3 | |
| Drumalee Court | 10 C3 | |
| Drumalee Drive | 10 C3 | |
| Drumalee Grove | 10 C3 | |
| Drumalee Park | 10 C3 | |
| Drumalee Road | 10 C3 | |
| Drumcliffe Drive | 10 C1 | |
| Drumcliffe Road | 9 B1 | |
| Drumcondra | 4 D2 | |
| Drumcondra Park | 12 D2[1] | |
| Drumcondra Rd Lwr | 4 D3/12 C1 | |
| Drumcondra Rd Upr | 4 D3 | |
| Drummond Place | 27 B3[4] | |
| Drury Street | 20 C3 | |
| Dufferin Avenue | 27 A2 | |
| Duke Lane Lower | 20 C3 | |
| Duke Lane Upper | 20 C3 | |
| Duke Row | 13 A3[4] | |
| Duke Street | 20 C3 | |
| Dunard Avenue | 9 A2 | |
| Dunard Court | 9 B2 | |
| Dunard Drive | 9 B2 | |
| Dunard Park | 9 B2 | |
| Dunard Road | 9 B2 | |
| Dunard Walk | 9 B2 | |
| Duncan Court | 8 D3[1] | |
| Dunluce Road | 8 C2 | |
| Dunmanus Road | 1 B3 | |
| Dunne Street | 13 A3 | |
| Dunseverick Road | 7 B3 | |
| Durham Road | 31 B2 | |
| Earl Place | 20 C1 | |
| Earl Street North | 20 C1 | |
| Earl Street South | 19 A3 | |
| Earls Court | 9 B2 | |
| Earlsfort Terrace | 28 D2 | |
| East Point Business Park | 14 D2 | |
| East Road | 22 C1 | |
| East Road (East Wall) | 14 C3 | |
| East Wall | 14 C3 | |
| East Wall Road | 14 C2 | |
| East Wall Rd (North Wall) | 22 D1 | |
| Eastmoreland La | 29 B2 | |
| Eastmoreland Pl | 29 B2[1] | |
| Ebenezer Terrace | 26 C1 | |
| Eblana Villas | 21 B3 | |
| Eccles Court | 12 C2 | |
| Eccles Place | 12 C2 | |
| Eccles Street | 11 B2 | |
| Echlin Street | 18 D3 | |
| Eden Quay | 20 D2 | |
| Edgewood | 4 D3[1] | |
| Elgin Road | 29 B2 | |
| Elizabeth Street | 12 D1 | |
| Ellesmere Avenue | 10 C2 | |
| Ellford Terrace | 26 D2[3] | |
| Ellis Court | 18 D2[6] | |
| Ellis Quay | 18 D2 | |
| Ellis Street | 18 D2 | |
| Elm Mount Avenue | 6 D1 | |
| Elm Mount Court | 7 A1 | |
| Elm Mount Drive | 7 A1 | |
| Elm Mount Road | 7 A1 | |
| Elm Road | 6 D1 | |
| Ely Place | 28 D1 | |
| Ely Place Upper | 28 D1[2] | |
| Emerald Cottages | 30 C1[2] | |
| Emerald Place | 21 A1 | |
| Emerald Square | 26 C1 | |
| Emerald Street | 21 B1 | |
| Emerald Terrace | 26 D1 | |
| Emmet Road | 17 A3 | |
| Emmet Street (Inchicore) | 12 D2 | |
| Emmet Street (Harold's Cross) | 27 A3 | |
| Emor Street | 27 B2 | |
| Emorville Avenue | 27 B2 | |
| Empress Place | 13 A3 | |
| Engine Alley | 19 A3[17] | |
| Ennafort Court | 8 D1 | |
| Ennafort Park | 8 D1 | |
| Ennafort Road | 8 D1 | |
| Ennaville Road | 13 B2 | |
| Ennis Grove | 30 D1 | |
| Enniskerry Road | 11 B1 | |
| Erne Place | 21 A3 | |
| Erne Place Little | 21 A3 | |
| Erne Place Lower | 21 A2 | |
| Erne Street Lower | 21 A2 | |
| Erne Street Upper | 21 A3 | |
| Erne Terrace Front | 21 A3 | |
| Erne Terrace Rere | 21 A3 | |
| Erris Road | 10 C1 | |
| Esmond Avenue | 13 B1 | |
| Essex Gate | 19 B2[1] | |
| Essex Quay | 19 B2 | |
| Essex Street E | 20 C2 | |
| Essex Street W | 19 B2 | |
| Estate Cottages | 29 B1 | |
| Estate Cottages (Ballsbridge) | 30 C2[6] | |
| Eugene Street | 26 D1 | |

| | | |
|---|---|---|
| Eustace Street | 20 C2 | |
| Everton Avenue | 10 C2 | |
| Ewington Lane | 18 C3 | |
| Exchange Street Lwr | 19 B2 | |
| Exchange Street Upr | 19 B2[2] | |
| Exchequer Street | 20 C3 | |
| Fade Street | 20 C3 | |
| Fairfield Avenue | 13 B3 | |
| Fairfield Road | 3 B3 | |
| Fairview | 14 C1 | |
| Fairview Ave Lwr | 13 B1 | |
| Fairview Ave Upr | 14 C1 | |
| Fairview Green | 13 B1 | |
| Fairview Passage | 13 B1 | |
| Fairview Strand | 13 B1 | |
| Fairview Terrace | 13 B1 | |
| Faith Avenue | 13 B2 | |
| Farney Park | 31 A2 | |
| Father Matthew Sq | 19 A1[4] | |
| Father Scully Hse | 12 D3[17] | |
| Fatima Mansions | 26 C1[3] | |
| Faussagh Avenue | 1 B3 | |
| Faussagh Road | 10 D1 | |
| Fenian Street | 21 A3 | |
| Ferguson Road | 4 C2 | |
| Ferrymans Crossing | 21 B1 | |
| Fertullagh Road | 10 D1[1] | |
| Findlater Place | 20 C1[1] | |
| Findlater Street | 18 C1 | |
| Fingal Place | 10 D3 | |
| Finglas Road | 2 D2 | |
| Finglas Road Old | 2 D1 | |
| Finglas Street | 26 D1 | |
| Finn Street | 18 C1 | |
| First Avenue | 21 B1 | |
| Fishamble Street | 19 B2 | |
| Fisherman's Wharf | 22 D2[1] | |
| Fitzgerald Street | 27 B3[2] | |
| Fitzgibbon Lane | 12 D2 | |
| Fitzgibbon Street | 12 D2 | |
| Fitzroy Avenue | 12 D2 | |
| Fitzwilliam Court | 28 D1[1] | |
| Fitzwilliam Lane | 29 A1 | |
| Fitzwilliam Place | 28 D2 | |
| Fitzwilliam Pl Little | 29 A1[3] | |
| Fitzwilliam Pl Nth | 19 A1[1] | |
| Fitzwilliam Quay | 22 D3 | |
| Fitzwilliam Sq E | 29 A1 | |
| Fitzwilliam Sq N | 29 A1 | |
| Fitzwilliam Sq S | 28 D1 | |
| Fitzwilliam Sq W | 28 D1 | |
| Fitzwilliam Street | 22 D3 | |
| Fitzwilliam St. Lwr | 29 A1 | |
| Fitzwilliam St. Upr. | 29 A1 | |
| Flag Alley | 19 A3[16] | |
| Fleet Street | 20 C2 | |
| Fleming Road | 4 C2 | |
| Fleming's Place | 29 A2 | |
| Florence Street | 27 B2[4] | |
| Foley Street | 20 D1 | |
| Fontenoy Street | 11 B3 | |
| Forbes Lane | 26 D1 | |
| Forbes Street | 21 B2 | |
| Fortescue Lane | 28 C3 | |
| Forth Road | 14 C3 | |
| Fortview Avenue | 16 D2 | |
| Foster Place North | 13 A2[11] | |
| Foster Place South | 20 C2 | |
| Foster Terrace | 13 A2 | |
| Fountain Place | 19 A1 | |
| Fountain Road | 17 B1 | |
| Fourth Avenue | 21 B1 | |
| Fownes St Lwr | 20 C2[7] | |
| Fownes St Upr | 20 C2 | |
| Foyle Road | 5 B3 | |
| Francis Street | 19 A3 | |
| Frankfort Cottages | 13 A3 | |
| Frederick Court | 12 C3[4] | |
| Frederick Lane N | 12 C3[7] | |
| Frederick Lane S | 20 D3 | |
| Frederick St Nth | 12 C3 | |
| Frederick St Sth | 20 D3 | |
| French Mullen Flats | 28 C2[8] | |
| Frenchman's Lane | 20 D1[1] | |
| Friary Avenue | 19 A1 | |
| Friary Grove | 19 A1[7] | |
| Fumbally Lane | 27 B1 | |
| Furry Park Court | 8 C2 | |
| Furry Park Road | 8 C2 | |
| Gaelic Street | 13 B3 | |
| Galmoy Road | 10 D1 | |
| Galtymore Drive | 25 A2 | |
| Galtymore Road | 25 A2 | |
| Gandon Hall | 20 D1[8] | |
| Garda Terrace | 18 C1 | |
| Garden Lane | 19 A3 | |
| Garden Terrace | 27 A2[6] | |
| Garden View | 28 C3[5] | |
| Gardiner Lane | 12 D3 | |
| Gardiner Place | 12 C3 | |
| Gardiner Row | 12 C3[5] | |
| Gardiner St Lwr | 20 D1 | |
| Gardiner St Mid | 12 D3 | |
| Gardiner St Upr | 12 C2 | |
| Gartan Avenue | 12 C1 | |
| Geoffrey Keating Rd | 27 A1[3] | |
| George Reynolds Flats | 22 D3[17] | |
| George's Hill | 19 B1 | |
| George's Lane | 19 A1 | |
| George's Place | 12 C2[12] | |
| George's Quay | 20 D2 | |
| George's St Gt N | 12 C3 | |
| George's St Gt S | 20 C3 | |
| George's Wharf | 11 B2[12] | |
| Gerald Street | 22 C3 | |
| Geraldine Street | 11 B2 | |
| Gilbert Road | 27 A2 | |
| Gilford Avenue | 31 B3 | |
| Gilford Court | 31 A2 | |
| Gilford Drive | 31 A3 | |
| Gilford Park | 31 A3 | |
| Gilford Road | 31 A2 | |
| Gilford Terrace | 31 B3 | |
| Glandore Road | 5 B2 | |
| Glasnevin | 3 B2 | |
| Glasnevin Court | 2 C1 | |
| Glasnevin Downs | 2 D1 | |
| Glasnevin Hill | 3 B2 | |
| Glasnevin Ind Est | 2 C2 | |
| Glasnevin Oaks | 2 D1 | |
| Glasnevin Woods | 2 C1 | |
| Glenard Avenue | 10 C2 | |
| Glenarm Avenue | 4 D3 | |
| Glenbeigh Park | 9 B2 | |
| Glenbeigh Road | 10 C2 | |
| Glencar Road | 9 B3 | |
| Glendalough Road | 4 C3 | |
| Glendinning Lane | 20 C3[10] | |
| Glenealy Road | 26 C3 | |
| Glengarriff Crescent | 12 C3 | |
| Glengarriff Parade | 12 C2 | |
| Glenmalure Park | 25 B1 | |
| Glenmore Road | 9 B2 | |
| Gloucester Diamond | 11 D3[13] | |
| Gloucester Lane | 12 D3[8] | |
| Gloucester Pl Lwr | 12 D3[9] | |
| Gloucester Pl Upr | 12 D3 | |
| Gloucester St Sth | 21 A2 | |
| Glovers Alley | 20 C3 | |
| Glovers Court | 20 C3[16] | |
| Godfrey Place | 10 C3 | |
| Golden Lane | 19 B3 | |
| Goldenbridge Ave | 25 A1 | |
| Goldsmith Street | 11 B2 | |
| Gordon Place | 28 C2[5] | |
| Gordon Street | 22 C3 | |
| Gortbeg Avenue | 1 B1 | |
| Gortbeg Drive | 1 B1 | |
| Gortbeg Park | 1 B1 | |
| Gortbeg Road | 1 B1 | |
| Gortmore Park | 1 B1 | |
| Grace Park Avenue | 5 A3 | |
| Grace Pk Gardens | 5 A3 | |
| Grace Park Heights | 5 B1 | |
| Grace Pk Meadows | 6 C1 | |

| | | |
|---|---|---|
| Grace Park Road | 5 | B1 |
| Grace Park Terrace | 5 | B2 |
| Gracefield Avenue | 8 | D1 |
| Grafton Street | 20 | C3 |
| Graham's Row | 11 | B3⁵ |
| Granby Lane | 11 | B3 |
| Granby Place | 20 | C1 |
| Granby Row | 11 | B3 |
| Grand Canal Place | 18 | D3 |
| Grand Canal Quay | 21 | B3 |
| Grand Canal St Lwr | 21 | B3 |
| Grand Canal St Upr | 29 | B1 |
| Grand Canal View | 25 | A1 |
| Grand Parade | 28 | D2 |
| Grangegorman Lwr | 19 | A1 |
| Grangegorman Upr | 11 | A3 |
| Grangegorman Villas | 11 | A3² |
| Granite Place | 30 | C3³ |
| Grant's Row | 21 | A3 |
| Grantham Place | 28 | C2 |
| Grantham Street | 27 | B2 |
| Grattan Court East | 29 | B1³ |
| Grattan Hall | 29 | B1⁷ |
| Grattan Parade | 12 | C1 |
| Grattan Place | 21 | B3 |
| Gray Square | 19 | A3² |
| Gray Street | 19 | A3 |
| Great Western Ave | 11 | A2 |
| Great Western Sq | 11 | A2 |
| Great Western Villas | 11 | A2 |
| Greek Street | 19 | B2 |
| Green Street | 19 | B1 |
| Green Street East | 22 | C2 |
| Green Street Little | 19 | B1 |
| Greenfield Place | 27 | B3¹ |
| Greenmount Ave | 27 | A3 |
| Greenmount Court | 27 | A3 |
| Greenmount Lane | 27 | A3 |
| Greenmount Square | 27 | A3² |
| Greenore Terrace | 21 | B3² |
| Greenville Avenue | 27 | A2 |
| Greenville Parade | 27 | A2¹ |
| Greenville Place | 27 | A2⁷ |
| Greenville Terrace | 27 | A2 |
| Grenville Lane | 12 | C3 |
| Grenville Street | 12 | C3 |
| Griffith Avenue (Finglas) | 3 | A1 |
| Griffith Avenue (Marino) | 5 | B2 |
| Griffith Avenue (Whitehall) | 4 | C1 |
| Griffith Court | 5 | B3 |
| Griffith Downs | 5 | A1 |
| Griffith Lawns | 4 | C1 |
| Griffith Square | 27 | A2⁵ |
| Griffith Vale | 5 | B2 |
| Grosvenor Court | 8 | C3 |
| Grove Avenue | 27 | B3⁵ |
| Grove Park | 27 | B3 |
| Grove Road | 27 | B3 |
| Guild Street | 21 | B1 |
| Guildford Place | 13 | A3¹ |
| Haddington Place | 29 | B1 |
| Haddington Road | 29 | B1 |
| Haddington Way East | 30 | C1⁷ |
| Haddon Court | 15 | B2² |
| Haddon Park | 15 | A1 |
| Haddon Road | 15 | B1 |
| Hagan's Court | 29 | A1 |
| Halliday Road | 18 | D1 |
| Halliday Square | 18 | C1 |
| Halpin's Row | 13 | A3¹¹ |
| Halston Street | 19 | B1 |
| Hamilton Court | 19 | B2⁵ |
| Hamilton Street | 26 | D1 |
| Hammond Lane | 19 | A2 |
| Hammond Street | 27 | A1 |
| Hampstead Park | 4 | C1 |
| Hampton Court | 29 | B3⁴ |
| Hampton Estate | 8 | D3 |
| Hampton Green | 9 | A1 |
| Hanbury Lane | 19 | A3 |
| Hanover Court | 19 | B3¹⁴ |
| Hanover Lane | 19 | B3 |
| Hanover Quay | 22 | C2 |
| Hanover Square | 19 | B3 |
| Hanover St E | 21 | A2 |
| Hanover St W | 19 | A3⁹ |
| Harbour Court | 20 | D1 |
| Harcourt Green | 28 | C2¹⁵ |
| Harcourt Lane | 28 | C2¹⁰ |
| Harcourt Road | 28 | C2 |
| Harcourt Street | 28 | C1 |
| Harcourt Terrace | 28 | D2 |
| Hardiman Road | 4 | C2 |
| Hardwicke Arch | 12 | C3² |
| Hardwicke Lane | 12 | C3³ |
| Hardwicke Place | 12 | C3⁶ |
| Hardwicke Street | 12 | C3 |
| Harman Street | 26 | D1 |
| Harmony Row | 21 | A3 |
| Harold Bridge Court | 27 | A3 |
| Harold Road | 18 | D1 |
| Harolds Cross | 26 | D3 |
| Harolds Cross Cotts | 27 | A3⁵ |
| Harolds Cross Rd | 27 | A3 |
| Haroldville Avenue | 26 | C1 |
| Harrington Street | 27 | B2 |
| Harry Court | 27 | B1⁷ |
| Harry Street | 20 | C3¹ |
| Harty Place | 27 | B1 |
| Hastings Street | 22 | C3 |
| Hatch Lane | 28 | D2 |
| Hatch Place | 28 | D2 |
| Hatch Street Lower | 28 | D2 |
| Hatch Street Upper | 28 | C2 |
| Hatters Lane | 27 | A3¹ |
| Havelock Square | 30 | C1 |
| Havelock Terrace | 30 | D1¹ |
| Haverty Road | 14 | C1 |
| Hawkins Street | 20 | D2 |
| Hawthorn Avenue | 13 | B3 |
| Hawthorn Terrace | 13 | B3 |
| Haymarket | 19 | A2 |
| Hazel Road | 6 | D1 |
| Healy Street | 12 | D3 |
| Hendrick Lane | 18 | D2⁵ |
| Hendrick Place | 18 | D2² |
| Henrietta House | 19 | B1⁵ |
| Henrietta Lane | 11 | B3 |
| Henrietta Place | 19 | B1 |
| Henrietta Street | 19 | B1 |
| Henry Place | 20 | C1 |
| Henry Street | 20 | C1 |
| Hepenstal Terrace | 31 | B2¹ |
| Herbert Cottages | 30 | C2⁴ |
| Herbert Court | 31 | A3 |
| Herbert Lane | 29 | A1 |
| Herbert Park | 30 | C3 |
| Herbert Park Lane | 30 | C3 |
| Herbert Place (Baggot Street) | 29 | A1 |
| Herbert Place (Irishtown) | 22 | D3⁴ |
| Herbert Road | 30 | D2 |
| Herbert Street | 29 | A1 |
| Herberton Drive | 26 | C2 |
| Herberton Park | 25 | B2 |
| Herberton Road | 25 | B1 |
| Heytesbury Lane | 29 | B3 |
| Heytesbury Street | 27 | B2 |
| Hibernian Avenue | 13 | B3 |
| High Street | 19 | B3 |
| Hill Street | 12 | C3 |
| Hogan Place | 21 | A3 |
| Holles Place | 21 | A3 |
| Holles Row | 21 | A3 |
| Holles Street | 21 | A3 |
| Holly Road | 6 | D2 |
| Hollybank Road | 4 | C3 |
| Hollybrook Court | 15 | A1³ |
| Hollybrook Ct Dr | 15 | A1² |
| Hollybrook Grove | 14 | D1 |
| Hollybrook Park | 7 | A3 |

| | | | | | | |
|---|---|---|---|---|---|---|
| Hollybrook Road | 15 A1 | James's Place E | 29 A1 | King Street North | 19 A1 |
| Holycross Avenue | 12 D1 | James's Street | 18 C3 | King Street South | 20 C3 |
| Holyrood Castle | 31 A3¹ | James's Street E | 29 A1 | King's Avenue | 13 A2¹⁶ |
| Holyrood Park | 31 A3 | James's Street N | 13 B2⁶ | Kingram Place | 28 D2 |
| Home Farm Park | 4 D2 | Janeville | 27 B2⁷ | Kings Court | 10 D3³ |
| Home Farm Road | 4 C1 | Jervis Lane Lower | 19 B2 | Kings Inns Court | 11 B3¹³ |
| Homelee | 30 D2³ | Jervis Lane Upper | 19 B1 | Kingsland Pk Ave | 27 B2³ |
| Hope Avenue | 13 B2 | Jervis Street | 19 B1 | Kingsland Parade | 27 B3 |
| Hope Street | 22 C3 | John Dillion Street | 19 B3 | Kippure Park | 1 A1 |
| Hospital Lane | 17 A2³ | John Field Road | 19 B3⁶ | Kirkwood | 31 A3 |
| Hotel Yard | 20 C1 | John Street South | 27 A1 | Kirwan Street | 18 D1 |
| Houghton Terrace | 18 D1¹ | John Street West | 19 A3 | Kirwan St Cotts | 10 D3 |
| Howard Street | 22 C3 | John's Lane | 19 A3 | Knightsbridge | 15 B1³ |
| Howth Rd | 7 B3 | John's Lane East | 19 B3 | Knocknarea Avenue | 25 A3 |
| (Clontarf) | | John's Street North | 18 D2⁴ | Knocknarow Tce | 17 B3¹¹ |
| Howth Rd | 6 D3 | Johnson Court | 20 C3 | Kyle-Clare Road | 23 A3¹ |
| (Fairview) | | Johnson Place | 20 C3¹² | La Vista Avenue | 7 B1 |
| Howth Rd | 8 C2 | Jones's Road | 12 D2 | Lad Lane | 29 A1 |
| (Killester) | | Josephine Avenue | 12 C2¹⁰ | Lad Lane Upper | 29 A2 |
| Hume Street | 28 D1 | Joy Street | 22 C3 | Lady's Lane | 17 A3 |
| Huxley Crescent | 26 D1² | Joyce Road | 4 C2 | Lagan Road | 1 B1 |
| Hyacinth Street | 13 B3 | Kearn's Place | 17 A3⁴ | Lamb Alley | 19 A3 |
| Hybreasal | 25 A1¹ | Keeper Road | 25 B2 | Lambay Road | 4 C1 |
| Imaal Road | 10 D2 | Kelly's Lane | 11 B2⁶ | Lambourne Village | 15 B1⁴ |
| Inchicore Road | 17 B3 | Kelly's Row | 12 C2 | Langan Road | 2 B2 |
| Infirmary Road | 17 B1 | Kenmare Parade | 12 C1¹ | Langrishe Place | 12 D3¹⁵ |
| Ingram Road | 27 A2 | Kerlogue Road | 23 A3 | Lansdowne Cres | 30 C1⁴ |
| Innisfallen Parade | 12 C2 | Kevin Barry Flats | 19 A1⁸ | Lansdowne Gdns | 30 C2² |
| Inns Quay | 19 A2 | Kevin Street Lower | 27 B1 | Lansdowne Hall | 30 D1² |
| Inver Road | 9 B1 | Kevin Street Upper | 27 B1 | Lansdowne Lane | 30 C1 |
| Inverness Road | 13 B1 | Kevins Avenue | 27 B1² | Lansdowne Park | 30 C1 |
| Iona Crescent | 3 B3 | Kickham Road | 25 A1 | Lansdowne Road | 30 C2 |
| Iona Drive | 4 C3 | Kilalla Road | 1 B3 | Lansdowne Square | 30 D2 |
| Iona Park | 3 B3 | Kilbride Road | 7 B2 | Lansdowne Terrace | 30 C1¹ |
| Iona Road | 3 B3 | Kildare Place | 20 D3³ | Lansdowne Village | 30 D1 |
| Iona Villas | 4 C3 | Kildare Street | 20 D3 | Lansdowne Villas | 30 C1³ |
| Irishtown | 31 A1 | Kilkieran Court | 1 B3 | Lawrence Grove | 7 A3 |
| Irishtown Road | 22 D3 | Kilkieran Road | 1 B3 | Le Vere Terrace | 27 A3⁴ |
| Irvine Cottages | 22 C1² | Killan Road | 22 C1 | Lea Crescent | 31 B2 |
| Irvine Terrace | 22 C1 | Killarney Avenue | 13 A2⁷ | Lea Road | 31 B2 |
| Irwin Court | 17 B3³ | Killarney Parade | 12 C2 | Leahy's Terrace | 31 A1 |
| Irwin Street | 17 B3⁴ | Killarney Street | 13 A3 | Lee Road | 2 C2 |
| Island Street | 18 D2 | Killester | 8 C1 | Leeson Close | 28 D2 |
| Island Villa | 21 B3¹ | Killester Avenue | 7 A1/7 B2 | Leeson Lane | 28 D1 |
| Islandbridge | 17 A2 | Killester Court | 7 B1 | Leeson Park | 29 A3 |
| Islandbridge Court | 17 A2² | Killester Park | 7 B1 | Leeson Park Ave | 29 A3 |
| Isolda Road | 23 A3 | Kilmainham | 17 A3 | Leeson Place | 28 D2 |
| Ivar Street | 18 D1 | Kilmainham Lane | 17 B3 | Leeson Street Lwr | 28 D1 |
| Iveagh Buildings | 19 B3¹¹ | Kilmainham Village | 18 C3² | Leeson Street Upr | 29 A2 |
| (Bride Rd) | | Kinahan Street | 18 C1 | Leeson Village | 29 A3 |
| Iveagh Buildings | 27 B1³ | Kincora Avenue | 15 B1 | Leeson Walk | 28 D3 |
| (Kevin St Upr) | | Kincora Drive | 15 B1 | Leinster Avenue | 13 B2 |
| Iveagh Gardens | 25 A3 | Kincora Grove | 15 B1 | Leinster Lane | 20 D3 |
| Ivetta Terrace | 4 D3³ | Kincora Park | 16 C1 | Leinster Market | 20 D2⁶ |
| Ivy Terrace | 26 D1 | Kincora Road | 16 C1 | Leinster Street E | 13 B2⁵ |

Leinster Street N 11 A1
Leinster Street S 20 D3
Leitrim Place 29 B7
Leix Road 10 D2
Lemon Street 20 C3
Lennox Place 27 B2
Lennox Street 28 C2
Lennox Terrace 28 C2[12]
Leo Avenue 12 C2[11]
Leo Street 12 C2
Leslie's Building 11 A2
Leukos Road 23 A3
Liberty House 12 D3[11]
Liberty Lane 28 C1
Liberty Square 19 A3[12]
Library View Tce 11 B2[1]
Liffey Street Lower 20 C2
Liffey Street Upper 20 C1
Liffey Street West 18 D2
Lime Street 21 A2
Limekiln Lane 27 A3
Lincoln Lane 19 A2[3]
Lincoln Place 20 D3
Lindsay Road 11 B1
Linenhall Parade 19 B1
Linenhall Street 19 B1[4]
Linenhall Terrace 19 B1
Lisburn Street 19 B1
Liscannor Road 1 B3
Lissadel Avenue 25 A3
Lissadel Court 25 A3
Lissadel Drive 25 A2
Lissenfield 29 C3[2]
Little Britain Street 19 B1
Little Mary Street 19 B2
Litton Lane 20 C2[1]
Lombard Court 21 A2[3]
Lombard Street E 21 A2
Lombard Street W 27 B2
Lomond Avenue 5 B3
Londonbridge Drive 30 D1
Londonbridge Road 30 D1
Long Lane 11 B3
Long Lane Close 27 B1[9]
Long's Place 18 D3
Longford Lane 20 C3[8]
Longford St Great 19 B3[7]
Longford St Little 20 C3[7]
Longwood Avenue 27 B2
Lord Edward Court 19 B3[12]
Lord Edward Street 19 B3
Lord's Walk 9 A3
Loreto Road 26 D1
Lorne Terrace 17 B3[14]
Lotts 20 C2

Lourdes House 12 D3[14]
Lourdes Road 26 C1
Love Lane East 29 B1[2]
Luby Road 17 A3
Luke Street 20 D2
Lullymore Terrace 26 D2
Lurgan Street 19 B1[1]
Lynch's Place 11 B2[3]
Lynton Court 30 D3[2]
Mabbot Lane 20 D1
Mabel Street 12 D1
Macken Street 21 B3
Macken Villa 21 B3
Mackie's Place 28 D1
Mackie's Place 28 D1[3]
Madden Road 27 A1
Madison Road 25 B1
Magdalen Terrace 22 D3[7]
Magennis Place 21 A2
Magennis Square 21 A2[1]
Malachi Place 13 B3[1]
Malachi Road 18 D1
Malahide Road 7 A1
(Donnycarney)
Malahide Road 14 C1
(Fairview)
Malahide Road 6 D3
(Marino)
Mallin Avenue 26 C1
Malone Gardens 30 C1
Malpas Court 27 B1[4]
Malpas Street 27 A1
Malpas Terrace 27 B1
Mander's Terrace 28 D3[3]
Mannix Road 4 C3
Manor Place 18 D1
Manor Street 18 D1
Margaret Place 30 C1
Marguerite Road 3 B3
Marine Drive 31 A2
Mariners Port 21 A1
Marino 5 B3
Marino Avenue 6 D3
Marino Crescent 14 C1
Marino Green 6 C3
Marino Mart 14 C1
Marino Park 6 C3
Marino Park Ave 14 C1
Marion Villas 26 D1
Mark's Alley West 19 A3
Mark's Lane 21 A2
Market Street South 18 D3
Marks Street 20 D2
Marlborough Court 20 D1[10]
Marlborough Mews 10 C3

Marlborough Place 20 D1[4]
Marlborough Road 10 C3
Marlborough Street 20 C1
Marmion Court 19 A1[6]
Marne Villas 11 A3
Marrowbone Lane 18 D3
Marrowbone La Blds 18 D3[3]
Marrowbone La Clo 18 D3[4]
Marshal Lane 18 D2
Marshalsea Lane 18 D3[2]
Martello View 31 B2
Martello Wood 31 B3
Martin Street 27 B2
Martin White Chalets 30 D2[2]
Mary Aikenhead Ho 18 C3[4]
Mary's Abbey 19 B2
Mary's Lane 19 B2
Matt Talbot Court 12 D3[1]
Mauncell Place 11 B3[14]
Maxwell Street 26 D1
May Lane 19 A2
May Park 7 A1
May Street 12 D2
Mayfield Road 25 B1
Mayor Street Lower 21 A1
Mayor Street Upper 22 C1
McCarthy Terrace 26 C1[1]
Mc Dowell Avenue 18 C3[1]
McKee Drive 9 B2
McKee Park 9 B2
McMahon Street 27 B2
Meades Terrace 21 A3
Meath Market 19 A3[13]
Meath Place 19 A3
Meath Square 19 A3[3]
Meetinghouse Lane 19 B2[3]
Meetinghouse Square 20 C2[13]
Melrose Avenue 13 B1
Memorial Road 20 D1
Mercer Street Lwr 20 C3
Mercer Street Upr 28 C1
Merchamp 16 D1
Merchant's Arch 20 C2[6]
Merchant's Quay 19 A2
Merchant's Road 14 D3
Merrion Close 21 A3[2]
Merrion Place 20 D3
Merrion Road 30 D3
Merrion Row 28 D1
Merrion Sq E 29 A1
Merrion Sq N 21 A3
Merrion Sq S 29 A1
Merrion Sq W 21 A3
Merrion St Lwr 21 A3
Merrion St Upr 28 D1

| | | |
|---|---|---|
| Merry Bush | 31 A2 | |
| Merton Avenue | 27 A2 | |
| Merton Park | 27 A2 | |
| Merville Avenue | 14 C1 | |
| Mespil Estate | 29 A2 | |
| Mespil Road | 29 A2 | |
| Middle Third | 8 C1 | |
| Military Road (Kilmainham) | 17 B3 | |
| Military Road (Rathmines) | 28 C3 | |
| Mill Brook | 17 B3[15] | |
| Mill Lane | 27 A1 | |
| Mill Street | 27 A1 | |
| Millbourne Avenue | 4 C3 | |
| Millbrook Terrace | 17 A3[7] | |
| Millmount Avenue | 4 C3 | |
| Millmount Place | 4 D3 | |
| Millmount Terrace | 4 D3 | |
| Millmount Villas | 4 C3 | |
| Misery Hill | 21 B2 | |
| Mitchell House | 29 A3[3] | |
| Moira Road | 18 C1 | |
| Moland Place | 20 D1[2] | |
| Molesworth Place | 20 D3[2] | |
| Molesworth Street | 20 D3 | |
| Molyneux Yard | 19 A3 | |
| Monck Place | 19 A3 | |
| Montague Court | 28 C1[3] | |
| Montague Lane | 28 C1 | |
| Montague Place | 28 C1 | |
| Montague Street | 28 C1 | |
| Montpelier Drive | 18 C1 | |
| Montpelier Gardens | 18 C1[2] | |
| Montpelier Hill | 18 C1 | |
| Montpelier Park | 18 C1 | |
| Moore Lane | 20 C1 | |
| Moore Street | 20 C1 | |
| Moracrete Cotts | 25 B3[1] | |
| Morehampton Lane | 29 B3 | |
| Morehampton Mews | 29 B3[2] | |
| Morehampton Sq | 29 B3[1] | |
| Morgan Place | 19 A2[4] | |
| Morning Star Ave | 19 A1 | |
| Morning Star Road | 26 C1 | |
| Morrogh Terrace | 5 B2[1] | |
| Moss Street | 20 D2 | |
| Mount Brown | 17 B3 | |
| Mount Drummond Avenue | 27 A3 | |
| Mount Drummond Square | 27 B3 | |
| Mount Prospect Lwr | 8 D3 | |
| Mount St Cres | 29 B1[4] | |
| Mount St Lower | 29 B1 | |
| Mount St Upper | 29 A1 | |
| Mount Temple Rd | 18 D1 | |
| Mountain View Ct | 12 D3[18] | |
| Mountjoy Parade | 12 D2[14] | |
| Mountjoy Place | 12 D3 | |
| Mountjoy Sq E | 12 D3 | |
| Mountjoy Sq N | 12 D2 | |
| Mountjoy Sq S | 12 D3 | |
| Mountjoy Sq W | 12 D3 | |
| Mountjoy Street | 11 B3 | |
| Mountjoy St Mid | 11 B3[9] | |
| Mountpleasant Ave Lower | 28 C3 | |
| Mountpleasant Ave Upper | 28 C3 | |
| Mountpleasant Pde | 28 C3[6] | |
| Mountpleasant Pl | 28 D3[2] | |
| Mountpleasant Sq | 28 C3 | |
| Mountpleasant Tce | 28 C3 | |
| Mountpleasant Tce Upper | 28 C3[8] | |
| Mountpleasant Villas | 28 D3[4] | |
| Mountshannon Rd | 25 B1 | |
| Mourne Rd | 25 A2 | |
| Moy Elta Road | 13 B3 | |
| Moyle Road | 2 C2 | |
| Muckross Parade | 12 C2[2] | |
| Mullinahack | 19 A2[9] | |
| Mulroy Road | 2 C3 | |
| Munster Street | 11 A1 | |
| Murtagh Road | 18 D1 | |
| Myrtle Street | 11 B3 | |
| Nassau Place | 20 D3[1] | |
| Nassau Street | 20 D3 | |
| Navan Road | 9 A1 | |
| Nelson Street | 11 B2 | |
| Nephin Road | 9 A1 | |
| Nerney's Court | 12 C3 | |
| New Bride Street | 27 B1 | |
| New Ireland Road | 25 B1 | |
| New Row South | 27 A1 | |
| New Row Square | 27 A1 | |
| New Street Grdns | 27 B1[8] | |
| New Street North | 19 A1 | |
| New Street South | 27 B1 | |
| New Wapping St | 22 C1 | |
| Newbridge Avenue | 30 D1 | |
| Newbridge Drive | 30 D1 | |
| Newcomen Avenue | 13 A2 | |
| Newcomen Court | 13 A2[7] | |
| Newgrange Road | 10 D1 | |
| Newgrove Avenue | 31 B2 | |
| Newmarket | 27 A1 | |
| Newmarket Street | 27 A1 | |
| Newport Street | 18 D3 | |
| Niall Street | 10 C3 | |
| Nicholas Avenue | 19 A1 | |
| Nicholas Street | 19 B3 | |
| Nore Road | 2 C2 | |
| Norfolk Road | 11 A1 | |
| Norseman Place | 18 D1 | |
| North Circular Road | 10 C3 | |
| North Circular Road | 12 D2 | |
| North Quay Ext | 22 D2 | |
| North Road | 9 A2 | |
| North Strand Road | 13 A3 | |
| North Wall | 21 B1 | |
| North Wall Quay | 21 B2 | |
| Northbrook Avenue | 28 D3 | |
| Northbrook Ave Lwr | 13 B2 | |
| Northbrook Ave Upr | 13 B2 | |
| Northbrook Lane | 28 D3 | |
| Northbrook Road | 28 D3 | |
| Northbrook Terrace | 13 B2[7] | |
| Northland Drive | 2 D1 | |
| Northland Grove | 2 D1 | |
| Northumberland Rd | 29 B1 | |
| Northumberland Sq | 20 D1[5] | |
| Norton's Avenue | 11 A2 | |
| Nottingham Street | 13 B2 | |
| O'Briens Place N | 4 C2 | |
| O'Briens Terrace | 11 B1 | |
| O'Carolan Road | 27 A1 | |
| O'Connell Avenue | 11 B2 | |
| O'Connell Gardens | 30 D1 | |
| O'Connell St Upr | 20 C1 | |
| O'Connell St Lwr | 20 C1 | |
| O'Curry Avenue | 27 A1[5] | |
| O'Curry Road | 27 A1 | |
| O'Daly Road | 4 C2 | |
| O'Devaney Gardens | 18 C1 | |
| O'Donovan Road | 27 A2 | |
| O'Hara Avenue | 27 B3 | |
| O'Leary Road | 25 A1 | |
| O'Neachtain Road | 4 C2[1] | |
| O'Neill's Buildings | 28 C1[4] | |
| O'Quinn Avenue | 18 C3 | |
| O'Rahilly House | 22 D3[11] | |
| O'Rahilly Parade | 20 C1 | |
| O'Reilly Avenue | 17 B3 | |
| O'Sullivan Avenue | 13 A2 | |
| Oak Road | 6 D2 | |
| Oakfield Place | 27 B2 | |
| Oaklands Drive | 31 A2 | |
| Oaklands Park | 30 D2 | |
| Oakley Park | 8 D3 | |
| Observatory Lane | 28 C3[1] | |
| Offaly Road | 10 D1 | |
| Olaf Road | 18 D1 | |

| | | | | | |
|---|---|---|---|---|---|
| Old Cabra Road | 10 C2 | Parliament Street | 19 B2 | Pine Road | 23 A3 |
| Old County Glen | 25 B3 | Parnell Avenue | 27 A3 | Pleasants Lane | 28 C1 |
| Old County Road | 25 B3 | Parnell Court | 27 A3 | Pleasants Place | 28 C1 |
| Old Kilmainham | 17 B3 | Parnell Place | 12 C3 | Pleasants Street | 27 B1 |
| Old Mill Court | 27 B1[1] | Parnell Road | 26 D2 | Polo Road | 9 A3 |
| Old Mountpleasant | 28 D3 | Parnell Sq East | 12 C3 | Poolbeg Street | 20 D2 |
| Oliver Plunkett Ave | 22 D3 | Parnell Sq North | 12 C3 | Poole Street | 19 A3[19] |
| Oliver Bond House | 19 A2[6] | Parnell Sq West | 12 C3 | Poplar Row | 13 B2 |
| Oliver Bond Street | 19 A2 | Parnell Street | 12 C3/20 C1 | Poplar Row (Apts) | 13 B2[4] |
| Ontario Terrace | 28 C3 | Patrick Street | 19 B3 | Portland Close | 13 A3[5] |
| Orchard Lane | 28 D3 | Pearse Grove | 21 B3[4] | Portland Court | 12 D2[3] |
| Orchard Road | 13 A1 | Pearse House | 21 A2 | Portland Place | 12 C2 |
| Orchard View | 11 A3[1] | Pearse Square | 21 B2 | Portland Row | 13 A3 |
| Oriel Hall | 21 A1 | Pearse Street | 20 D2 | Portland Square | 12 D2[8] |
| Oriel Place | 13 B3 | Pembroke Cottages | 22 D2 | Portland Street N | 12 D2 |
| Oriel Street Lower | 13 B3 | Pembroke Gardens | 29 B2 | Portland Street W | 18 D3 |
| Oriel Street Upper | 21 A1 | Pembroke Lane | 29 A1 | Portmahon Drive | 25 B1 |
| Ormeau Street | 22 C3[1] | Pembroke Park | 29 B3 | Portobello Harbour | 28 C2 |
| Ormond Place | 19 B2[4] | Pembroke Place | 28 D2[2] | Portobello Place | 28 C2[13] |
| Ormond Quay Lwr | 20 C2 | Pembroke Place | 30 C3[2] | Portobello Road | 27 B3 |
| Ormond Quay Upr | 19 B2 | (Ballsbridge) | | Portside Business C. | 14 C2 |
| Ormond Road | 4 D3 | Pembroke Road | 29 B2 | Portside Court | 14 C2 |
| Ormond Square | 19 B2 | Pembroke Road | 30 C1 | Power's Court | 29 B1 |
| Ormond Street | 27 A1 | Pembroke Row | 29 A1 | Power's Square | 19 B3[15] |
| Osbourne Terrace | 28 D3[8] | Pembroke Square | 21 B3 | Prebend Street | 19 A1 |
| Oscar Square | 27 A1 | Pembroke Street | 22 D3 | Preston Street | 13 A3[8] |
| Ossory Road | 13 B3 | Pembroke St Lwr | 28 D1 | Price's Lane | 20 C2 |
| Ostman Place | 18 D1 | Pembroke St Upr | 28 D1 | (Aston Quay) | |
| Oswald Road | 31 A1 | Penrose Street | 22 C3 | Price's Lane | 28 C3 |
| Oulton Park | 16 C1 | Percy Lane | 29 B1 | (Ranelagh) | |
| Our Lady's Close | 26 D1[5] | Percy Place | 29 B1 | Priestfield Cottages | 26 D2[1] |
| Our Lady's Road | 26 D1 | Peter Place | 28 C2 | Priestfield Drive | 26 D2[2] |
| Ovoca Road | 27 B2 | Peter Row | 28 C1 | Primrose Avenue | 11 B3 |
| Owens Avenue | 17 B3[7] | Peter Street | 19 B3 | Primrose Street | 11 B3[3] |
| Oxford Road | 28 D3 | Peterson's Court | 21 A2[2] | Prince of Wales Tce | 30 D3[1] |
| Oxmantown Lane | 19 A2 | Petrie Road | 27 A2 | Prince's St Sth | 21 A2 |
| Oxmantown Road | 10 C3 | Phibsboro | 11 A2 | Prince's St Nth | 20 C1 |
| Palace Street | 20 C2[12] | Phibsborough | 11 B2 | Prior Hall | 18 C3[3] |
| Palatine Square | 18 C1 | Phibsborough Ave | 11 A2 | Proby's Lane | 20 C1 |
| Palmerston Place | 11 B3 | Phibsborough Place | 11 B2[5] | Promenade Road | 15 A3 |
| Paradise Place | 11 B3 | Phibsborough Road | 11 B2 | Prospect Avenue | 3 B3 |
| Park Avenue | 31 A3 | Philipsburgh Ave | 5 B3/13 B1 | Prospect Road | 11 B1 |
| Park Avenue West | 18 C2[2] | Philipsburgh Terrace | 5 B3 | Prospect Square | 3 B3 |
| Park Court | 31 A3 | Philomena Terrace | 22 D3[5] | Prospect Terrace | 17 A3[6] |
| Park Lane | 31 A3 | Phoenix Court | 18 C1 | (Kilmainham) | |
| Park Lane East | 20 D2 | Phoenix Manor | 10 C3 | Prospect Terrace | 31 A1[4] |
| Park Mews | 29 B3 | Phoenix Street N | 19 A2 | (Sandymount) | |
| Park Place | 17 A2[1] | Pig Lane | 12 D3 | Prospect Way | 3 B3 |
| Park Springs | 9 A1 | Pigeon House Road | 24 C3 | Protestant Row | 28 C1[2] |
| Park Terrace | 19 A3[10] | Pigeon House Rd | 23 A2 | Proud's Lane | 28 C1 |
| Park View | 9 B2 | (Ringsend) | | Prussia Street | 10 D3 |
| Parkgate Street | 18 C2 | Pim Street | 18 D3 | Pyro Villas | 26 D1 |
| Parkview Court | 9 A2[1] | Pimlico | 19 A3 | Quarry Cottages | 7 B2[1] |
| Parkview Place | 22 D3[3] | Pimlico Cottages | 19 A3[18] | Quarry Road | 10 C1 |
| Parliament Row | 20 C2[10] | Pine Hurst | 9 B1 | Queen Street | 19 A2 |

| | | |
|---|---|---|
| Quinn's Lane | 28 D1 | |
| Raglan Lane | 29 B2 | |
| Raglan Road | 29 B2 | |
| Railway Cottages | 30 D2[1] | |
| Railway Street | 12 D3 | |
| Railway Terrace | 21 B3 | |
| Rainsford Avenue | 18 D3[1] | |
| Rainsford Street | 18 D3 | |
| Raleigh Square | 25 A3 | |
| Ranelagh | 28 D3 | |
| Ranelagh Avenue | 28 D3 | |
| Rath Row | 20 D2[2] | |
| Rathdown Road | 11 A2 | |
| Rathdown Square | 10 D3 | |
| Rathdrum Road | 26 C3 | |
| Rathlin Road | 4 C1 | |
| Rathmines | 27 C3 | |
| Rathmines Rd Lwr | 28 C3 | |
| Ratoath Estate | 1 A2 | |
| Ratoath Road | 1 A2 | |
| Ravensdale Road | 14 C3 | |
| Raymond Street | 27 A2 | |
| Red Cow Lane | 19 A1 | |
| Redmond's Hill | 28 C1 | |
| Reginald Square | 19 A3[4] | |
| Reginald Street | 19 A3 | |
| Rehoboth Avenue | 26 D2 | |
| Rehoboth Place | 26 C2 | |
| Reilly's Avenue | 26 C2 | |
| Reuben Avenue | 26 C1 | |
| Reuben Street | 26 C1 | |
| Rialto Buildings | 26 C1 | |
| Rialto Cottages | 25 B1 | |
| Rialto Drive | 25 B2 | |
| Rialto Place | 26 C1[4] | |
| Rialto Street | 26 C1 | |
| Richmond Avenue | 13 A1 | |
| Richmond Cottages | 13 A2[3] | |
| Richmond Cotts N | 13 A2 | |
| Richmond Crescent | 13 A2[2] | |
| Richmond Estate | 13 B1 | |
| Richmond Hill | 28 C3 | |
| Richmond Lane | 12 D2[12] | |
| Richmond Mews | 28 C3 | |
| Richmond Parade | 13 A2[10] | |
| Richmond Place | 28 C3 | |
| Richmond Pl Sth | 28 C2[9] | |
| Richmond Road | 4 D3/13 A1 | |
| Richmond Row | 28 C2 | |
| Richmond St Nth | 13 A2 | |
| Richmond St Sth | 28 C2 | |
| Richmond Villas | 28 C2[4] | |
| Ringsend | 22 D3 | |
| Ringsend Park | 22 D2 | |
| Ringsend Road | 22 C3 | |
| River Gardens | 3 B2 | |
| Riverston Abbey | 1 A2 | |
| Robert Place | 12 D1[1] | |
| Robert Street | 18 D3 | |
| Robert Street (Drumcondra) | 12 D1 | |
| Robert Street South | 18 D3 | |
| Roger's Lane | 28 D1 | |
| Roosevelt Cottages | 9 A1 | |
| Rope Walk Place | 22 D3 | |
| Rosary Road | 26 C1 | |
| Rosary Terrace | 22 D3 | |
| Rosedale Terrace | 27 B2[2] | |
| Rosemount | 7 A1 | |
| Rosemount Court | 17 A3[1] | |
| Rosemount Road | 11 A2 | |
| Rosemount Terrace | 18 D1 | |
| Rosevale Court | 8 D1 | |
| Rosevale Mansions | 8 D1 | |
| Ross Road | 19 B3 | |
| Ross Street | 10 C3 | |
| Rostrevor Terrace | 21 B3[3] | |
| Rothe Abbey | 25 A1 | |
| Rowerstown Lane | 17 A3[3] | |
| Royal Canal Bank | 11 B2 | |
| Royal Canal Court | 11 B2[13] | |
| Royal Canal Tce | 11 A3 | |
| Royse Road | 11 B1 | |
| Russell Avenue | 12 D2 | |
| Russell Ave East | 13 B3 | |
| Russell Street | 12 D2 | |
| Rutland Avenue | 26 C3 | |
| Rutland Cottages | 12 D3[4] | |
| Rutland Place North | 12 D3 | |
| Rutland Place West | 12 C3 | |
| Rutland St Lower | 12 D3 | |
| Rutledge Terrace | 26 D2 | |
| Ryder's Row | 19 B1 | |
| Sackville Avenue | 13 A2 | |
| Sackville Gardens | 13 A2[1] | |
| Sackville Place | 20 C1 | |
| St Agatha Court | 13 A3[10] | |
| St Aidan's Park | 6 C3 | |
| St Aidan's Pk Ave | 6 C3 | |
| St Aidan's Pk Rd | 14 C1 | |
| St Alban's Street | 27 A2 | |
| St Alphonsus Avenue | 12 C1[1] | |
| St Alphonsus Rd Lwr | 12 C1 | |
| St Alphonsus Rd Upr | 12 C1 | |
| St Andrews Lane | 20 C3[11] | |
| St Andrews Street | 20 C3 | |
| St Anne's Rd Nth | 12 C1 | |
| St Anne's Rd Sth | 26 D2 | |
| St Anthony's Place | 12 C3[1] | |
| St Anthony's Road | 26 C1 | |
| St Attracta Road | 2 C3 | |
| St Audoen's House | 19 A2[5] | |
| St Audoen's Tce | 19 A2 | |
| St Augustine Street | 19 A2 | |
| St Barnaba's Gdns | 13 B3 | |
| St Benedict's Gdns | 12 C2[4] | |
| St Brendan's Cotts | 22 D3 | |
| St Brendan's Road | 12 C1 | |
| St Bricin's Park | 18 C1 | |
| St Brigid's Avenue | 13 B2 | |
| St Brigid's Cotts | 13 B2[9] | |
| St Brigid's Court | 7 B1 | |
| St Brigid's Drive | 7 B1 | |
| St Brigid's Road | 8 C1 | |
| St Brigid's Rd Upr | 12 C1 | |
| St Catherine's Ave | 26 D2 | |
| St Catherine's La W | 19 A3 | |
| St Clare's Avenue | 27 A3 | |
| St Clement's Road | 12 C1[2] | |
| St Columba's Rd Lwr | 12 C1 | |
| St Columba's Rd Upr | 12 C1 | |
| St David's Court | 15 B1[5] | |
| St David's Terrace (Blackhorse Ave) | 10 C3 | |
| St David's Terrace (Glasnevin) | 3 B1 | |
| St David's Wood | 7 A1 | |
| St Declan's Road | 6 C3 | |
| St Declan's Terrace | 6 C3 | |
| St Eithne Road | 10 D1 | |
| St Elizabeth's Ct | 10 D2 | |
| St Finbar's Road | 2 C3 | |
| St Finbarr's Court | 1 B3[1] | |
| St Fintan Road | 10 D1 | |
| St Fintan Terrace | 2 D3 | |
| St Francis Square | 19 B3[1] | |
| St George's Ave | 12 D1 | |
| St Helena's Road | 1 B1 | |
| St Ignatius Avenue | 12 C2 | |
| St Ignatius Road | 12 C1 | |
| St Ita's Road | 3 B2[1] | |
| St James Place | 31 A2[4] | |
| St James's Avenue | 13 A2 | |
| St James's Avenue | 18 C3 | |
| St James's Terrace (Dolphin's Barn) | 26 C2 | |
| St James's Terrace (Sandymount) | 31 A1[1] | |
| St James's Walk | 26 C1 | |
| St Jarlath Road | 10 D1 | |
| St John's Avenue | 19 A3[5] | |
| St John's Cottages | 17 B3[2] | |
| St John's Court | 6 D2[1] | |
| St John's Rd West | 17 B2 | |
| St John's Street | 27 A1[1] | |

St John's Terrace 17 B3[12]
St John's Wood 15 B1[2]
St Joseph's Avenue 13 A1
  (Clonliffe Road)
St Joseph's Avenue 12 C1
  (Drumcondra)
St Joseph's Cotts 13 A3[13]
St Joseph's Court 10 D3[2]
St Joseph's Mansions 13 A3
St Joseph's Parade 11 B2
St Joseph's Place 11 B3[8]
  (Phibsborough)
St Joseph's Place 10 D3
  (Prussia Street)
St Joseph's Road 10 D3
St Joseph's Square 16 D2[2]
St Joseph's Street 12 C2[7]
St Joseph's Terrace 12 D2[13]
  (North Circular Rd)
St Joseph's Tce 13 B1[3]
  (Marino)
St Joseph's Tce 22 D3[12]
  (Ringsend)
St Joseph's Villas 13 A2[9]
St Kevin's Cotts 27 B2[1]
St Kevin's Parade 27 B2
St Kevin's Road 27 B3
St Laurence Place 11 B3[2]
St Laurence Pl E 21 B1[1]
St Lawrence Road 15 A1
St Lawrence's Court 7 A3
St Maignenn's Tce 17 B3[6]
St Malachy Road 4 C2
St Margaret's Ave 19 A3[6]
  (Pimlico)
St Margaret's Ave 26 D1[1]
  (Cork Street)
St Margaret's Ave N 12 D2[11]
St Margarets Tce 26 D1
St Mary's Ave Nth 11 B3[6]
St Mary's Lane 29 B1[5]
St Mary's Mansions 12 D3[10]
St Mary's Place Nth 11 B3
St Mary's Rd Nth 14 C3
St Mary's Rd Sth 29 B2
St Mary's Terrace 18 D1[3]
  (Arbour Hill)
St Mary's Terrace 11 B3
  (Phibsborough)
St Mary's Terrace 22 D3[14]
  (Ringsend)
St Michael's Close 19 B3[10]
St Michael's Hill 19 B3[8]
St Michael's Place 11 B3[15]
St Michael's Road 4 C2

St Michael's Tce 27 A1
St Michan's House 19 B2[6]
St Michan's Lane 19 B2[7]
St Michan's Street 19 B2
St Mobhi Boithrin 3 B1
St Mobhi Court 3 B1
St Mobhi Drive 3 B2
St Mobhi Grove 3 B2
St Mobhi Road 3 B2
St Mura's Terrace 13 B3[2]
St Nicholas Place 19 B3
St Patrick's Avenue 13 B2[3]
St Patrick's Close 27 B1
St Patrick's Parade 12 C1
St Patrick's Place 11 B3[1]
St Patrick's Road 12 C1
St Patrick's Terrace 12 D1[2]
  (Fitzroy Ave)
St Patrick's Terrace 12 D2[9]
  (Russell St)
St Patrick's Villas 22 D3
St Paul Street 19 A1
St Peter's Avenue 11 A2
St Peter's Court 11 B2[2]
St Peter's Road 11 A2
St Philomena's Rd 3 A3
St Stephen's Gn E 28 D1
St Stephen's Gn N 20 D3
St Stephen's Gn S 28 C1
St Stephen's Gn W 28 C1
St Teresa Place 3 B3
St Teresa Road 3 B3
St Teresa's Gdns 26 D2
St Thomas Road 27 A1
St Ultan's Flats 28 C2[8]
St Vincent's Court 6 C1[1]
St Vincent St Nth 11 B2[8]
St Vincent St Sth 27 B2
Saddlers Court 28 C3
Sampson's Lane 20 C1
Sandford Avenue 26 D2
Sandford Gardens 27 A2
Sandford Park 27 A2[2]
Sandwith St Lwr 21 A2
Sandwith St Upr 21 A3
Sandymount 31 A2
Sandymount Ave 30 D3
Sandymount Castle 31 A2[3]
Sandymount Cas Dr 31 A2
Sandymount Cas Pk 31 B2
Sandymount Cas Rd 31 A2
Sandymount Court 31 A1[2]
Sandymount Green 31 A2[2]
Sandymount Road 31 A1
Sarah Place 17 A2

Sarsfield Street 11 B2[9]
Sarsfield Quay 18 D2
School Street 18 D3
Schoolhouse Lane 20 D3
Schoolhouse La W 19 B3[3]
Seafield Avenue 16 D1
Seafield Court 16 C1[1]
Seafield Road East 16 D1
Seafield Road West 16 C1
Seafort Avenue 31 A2
Seafort Cottages 31 A2
Seafort Gardens 31 A1
Seafort Terrace 31 A2[1]
Seafort Villas 31 A2
Sean MacDermott St 12 D3
  Lower
Sean MacDermott St 12 D2
  Upper
Sean Moore Road 23 A3
Sean O'Casey Ave 12 D3
Seapoint Terrace 22 D3[15]
Seaview Ave E 14 C3
Seaview Ave Nth 15 A1
Second Avenue 21 B1
Selskar Terrace 28 D3
Serpentine Avenue 30 D3
Serpentine Park 30 D2
Serpentine Road 30 D2
Serpentine Terrace 30 D2
Seven Oaks 5 A1
Seville Place 12 B1/13 A3
Seville Terrace 13 A3
Shamrock Cottages 13 A3[3]
Shamrock Place 13 A3[2]
Shamrock Street 11 B3
Shamrock Terrace 13 A3
Shandon Crescent 10 D1
Shandon Drive 11 A1
Shandon Gardens 2 D3
Shandon Park 11 A1
Shandon Road 11 A1
Shanganagh Road 4 C3
Shannon Terrace 17 B3[5]
Shaw Street 20 D2
Shaw's Lane 30 C1
Shea's Court 10 D3[5]
Shelbourne Avenue 30 C2
Shelbourne Lane 30 C2[1]
Shelbourne Road 30 C1
Shellysbanks Road 24 C3
Shelmalier Road 14 C3
Shelmartin Avenue 5 B3
Shelmartin Terrace 5 B3
Sheriff Street Lower 21 A1
Sheriff Street Upper 21 B1

| | | | | | | | |
|---|---|---|---|---|---|---|---|
| Sherkin Gardens | 4 D1 | (Leeson Street) | | Swanard Court | 26 D3 |
| Sherrard Avenue | 12 C2 | Stable Lane | 19 A2 | Sweeney's Terrace | 27 A1 |
| Sherrard Court | 12 C2⁶ | (Arran Qy) | | Swift's Alley | 19 A3 |
| Sherrard St Lwr | 12 D2 | Stable Lane | 28 C1 | Swift's Row | 20 C2 |
| Sherrard St Upr | 12 C2 | (Harcourt St) | | Swilly Road | 9 B1 |
| Ship Street Great | 19 B3 | Stamer Street | 27 B2 | Sword Street | 18 C1 |
| Ship Street Little | 19 B3 | Stanhope Street | 19 A1² | Swords Road | 5 A1 |
| Shrewsbury | 31 A3 | Stanley Street | 19 A1 | Sybil Hill Road | 8 D2 |
| Sibthorpe Lane | 29 A3 | Steeven's Lane | 18 C2 | Sycamore Street | 20 C2 |
| Sigurd Road | 18 D1 | Stella Avenue | 4 C1 | Sydenham Road | 30 D3 |
| Simmon's Place | 12 D3² | Stella Gardens | 22 D3 | Synge Lane | 27 B2 |
| Simmonscourt Road | 30 D3 | Stephen Street | 20 C3 | Synge Place | 28 C2 |
| Simpson's Lane | 22 D3¹⁶ | Lower | | Synge Street | 28 C2 |
| Sion Hill Court | 5 B1 | Stephen Street | 19 B3 | Synnott Place | 12 C2 |
| Sion Hill Road | 5 B1 | Upper | | Synnott Row | 12 C2⁸ |
| Sir John Rogerson's | 21 B2 | Stephen's Lane | 29 A1 | Taaffe's Place | 13 B2 |
| Quay | | Stephens Place | 29 A1 | Talbot Lane | 20 D1⁷ |
| Sitric Place | 18 D1¹ | Stephens Road | 25 A1 | Talbot Place | 20 D1 |
| Sitric Road | 18 D1 | Stirrup Lane | 19 A1 | Talbot Street | 20 D1 |
| Skreen Road | 9 A1 | Stoke's Place | 28 C1 | Tangier Lane | 20 C3¹⁵ |
| Slade Row | 18 C1 | Stoney Road | 13 B2 | Tara Street | 20 D2 |
| Slane Road | 25 B3 | Stoneybatter | 18 D1 | Taylor's Lane | 18 D1 |
| Slaney Close | 2 C2 | Store Street | 20 D1 | Temple Bar | 20 C2 |
| Slaney Road | 2 C2 | Strand Road | 31 B2 | Temple Bar Square | 20 C2¹⁵ |
| Slemish Road | 9 A2 | Strand Street | 23 A3 | Temple Buildings | 11 B3¹⁰ |
| Slievenamon Road | 25 A1 | Strand Street Great | 19 B2 | Temple Cottages | 11 B3 |
| Smithfield | 19 A2 | Strand Street Little | 19 B2 | Temple Court | 18 C1 |
| Smithfield Terrace | 19 A1⁵ | Strandville Avenue | 13 B2 | Temple Lane North | 12 C3 |
| Somerset Street | 22 C3 | Strandville Ave E | 15 A1⁴ | Temple Lane South | 20 C2 |
| South Bank Road | 23 B3 | Strandville Ave E | 14 D1 | Temple Place | 28 D3 |
| South Circular Rd | 26 C2 | Strandville House | 15 A1¹ | Temple Street West | 18 C2 |
| (Dolphin's Barn) | | Strandville Place | 13 B2⁸ | Temple Villas | 18 C1³ |
| South Circular Rd | 17 A2 | Strangford Gardens | 13 B3 | Terminal Rd Nth | 24 D1 |
| (Islandbridge) | | Strangford Rd East | 13 B3 | Terminal Rd Sth | 24 D1 |
| South Circular Rd | 25 B1 | Strasburg Terrace | 22 D3⁸ | Terrace Place | 12 D3⁵ |
| (Kilmainham) | | Strongs Court | 20 C1² | The Anchorage | 22 C3³ |
| South Dock Place | 22 C3 | Suffolk Street | 20 C2 | The Appian Way | 29 A3 |
| South Dock Road | 22 C3 | Suir Road | 25 A1 | The Bramblings | 7 B2 |
| South Dock Street | 22 C3 | Sullivan Street | 17 B1¹ | The Cloisters | 5 A1 |
| South Link Road | 31 A1 | Summer Arch | 12 D2 | The Court | 15 A1 |
| South Lotts Road | 22 C3 | Summer Place | 12 D3 | The Crescent | 5 A1 |
| Spa Road | 9 A3 | Summer St North | 12 D3 | The Grove | 5 A1 |
| Spafield Terrace | 30 D3³ | Summer St South | 18 D3 | The Haven | 3 B1 |
| Spencer Dock | 21 B1 | Summerhill | 12 D3 | The Meadows | 8 D1 |
| Spencer Place | 13 B2¹¹ | Summerhill Parade | 13 A2 | The Mews | 7 B1 |
| Spencer Row | 20 D1³ | Summerhill Place | 12 D3 | The Mews | 15 B1 |
| Spencer St North | 13 B2 | Summerville | 16 C2 | The Orchard | 8 C1 |
| Spencer St South | 27 B2 | Sundrive Road | 25 B3 | The Paddocks | 25 A1 |
| Spencer Terrace | 26 D1³ | Susan Terrace | 27 A1 | (South Circular Rd) | |
| Spitalfields | 19 A3¹¹ | Susanville Road | 13 A1 | The Paddocks | 15 B1 |
| Spring Avenue | 13 A2 | Sussex Road | 29 A2 | The Pines | 8 C1 |
| Spring Garden La | 20 D2 | Sussex Terrace | 28 D2³ | The Square | 22 D3 |
| Spring Garden St | 13 A2 | Swan Alley | 19 A3 | The Square | 30 C1⁸ |
| Springfield | 9 A2 | Swan Grove | 28 D3 | The Stiles Road | 7 B3 |
| Stable Lane | 28 D1 | Swan Place | 29 A3 | The Sweepstakes | 30 C2⁷ |

| | | |
|---|---|---|
| he Turrets | 30 D2 | |
| he Village | 4 D1 | |
| he Willows | 2 D2 | |
| nird Avenue | 21 B1 | |
| homas Court | 18 D3 | |
| homas Davis St Sth | 19 A3 | |
| nomas Lane | 20 C1 | |
| homas St West | 18 D3 | |
| nompson's Cotts | 12 D3[3] | |
| nor Place | 18 C1[1] | |
| horncastle Street | 22 D2 | |
| horndale Drive | 7 A1 | |
| horndale Grove | 7 A1 | |
| hundercut Alley | 19 A1 | |
| olka Cottages | 2 D1 | |
| olka Estate Road | 2 D1 | |
| olka Quay Road | 23 A1 | |
| olka Road | 13 A1 | |
| olka Valley Road | 1 A1 | |
| om Clarke House | 13 A1[1] | |
| om Kelly Road | 28 C2 | |
| omar Court | 18 C1[4] | |
| orlogh Gardens | 13 B1 | |
| orlogh Parade | 5 B2[2] | |
| ower View Cotts | 3 A3 | |
| ownsend Street | 20 D2 | |
| raynor Place | 17 B3[13] | |
| rinity Square | 21 A2[4] | |
| rinity Street | 20 C2 | |
| rinity Terrace | 13 A2[13] | |
| ritonville Avenue | 31 A1 | |
| ritonville Close | 31 A1[3] | |
| ritonville Court | 31 A2 | |
| ritonville Crescent | 31 A1 | |
| ritonville Mews | 31 A1[5] | |
| ritonville Road | 30 D1 | |
| urvey Avenue | 17 A3[2] | |
| yrrel's Lane | 22 D3[9] | |
| yrrell Place | 12 D2[15] | |
| Ilster Street | 11 A1 | |
| lster Terrace | 13 A2[5] | |
| pper Cross Road | 25 B1 | |
| sher Street | 19 A2 | |
| sher's Island | 18 D2 | |
| sher's Lane | 19 A2[8] | |
| sher's Quay | 19 A2 | |
| alentia Parade | 12 C2 | |
| alentia Road | 4 C1 | |
| auxhall Avenue | 26 C1 | |
| avasour Square | 30 C1 | |
| enetian Hall | 8 C1 | |
| entry Drive | 1 A3 | |
| entry Park | 1 A3 | |
| entry Road | 1 B3 | |
| era Terrace | 4 C2[2] | |
| Vernon Avenue | 8 C2/16 D1 | |
| Vernon Court (Clontarf Road) | 16 D2 | |
| Vernon Court (Seafield Road) | 16 D1 | |
| Vernon Drive | 8 D2 | |
| Vernon Gardens | 16 D1 | |
| Vernon Grove | 16 D1 | |
| Vernon Heath | 8 D3 | |
| Vernon Park | 8 D3 | |
| Vernon Rise | 8 D2 | |
| Vernon Street | 27 B1 | |
| Veronica Terrace | 22 D3[6] | |
| Verschoyle Court | 29 B1 | |
| Verschoyle Place | 29 A1 | |
| Vicar Street | 19 A3 | |
| Victoria Cottages | 22 D3[13] | |
| Victoria Lane | 4 D3 | |
| Victoria Quay | 18 D2 | |
| Victoria Road | 15 B1 | |
| Victoria Street | 27 B2 | |
| Victoria Villas | 6 D3 | |
| Viking Harbour | 18 D2[3] | |
| Viking Place | 18 D1 | |
| Viking Road | 18 D1 | |
| Violet Hill Drive | 2 D1 | |
| Violet Hill Park | 2 D1 | |
| Violet Hill Road | 2 D1 | |
| Walker's Cottages | 28 C3 | |
| Walker's Court | 28 C3[7] | |
| Walnut Avenue | 4 D1 | |
| Walnut Lawn | 4 D1 | |
| Walnut Park | 4 D1 | |
| Walnut Rise | 4 D1 | |
| Walsh Road | 4 C2 | |
| Walworth Street | 27 B2[5] | |
| Ward's Hill | 27 A1 | |
| Warner's Lane | 28 D2 | |
| Warren Street | 27 B2 | |
| Warrenmount | 27 A1[9] | |
| Warrenmount Place | 27 A1[2] | |
| Warrenpoint | 15 B1[1] | |
| Warrington Lane | 29 B1 | |
| Warrington Place | 29 B1 | |
| Warwick Terrace | 29 A3[1] | |
| Washington Street | 27 A2 | |
| Waterfall Avenue | 5 A3 | |
| Waterloo Avenue | 13 B2 | |
| Waterloo Lane | 29 A3 | |
| Waterloo Road | 29 A3 | |
| Waterside Flats | 22 C3[2] | |
| Watkin's Buildings | 27 A1[6] | |
| Watling Street | 18 D2 | |
| Waverley Avenue | 13 B1 | |
| Weaver Lane | 11 B2[4] | |
| Weaver's Close | 27 A1[7] | |
| Weaver's Street | 27 A1 | |
| Weaver's Square | 27 A1[10] | |
| Wellesley Place | 12 D2[10] | |
| Wellington Lane | 29 B3 | |
| Wellington Place | 29 B3 | |
| Wellington Pl Nth | 11 B3[4] | |
| Wellington Quay | 20 C2 | |
| Wellington Road | 29 B2 | |
| Wellington Road (Phoenix Park) | 17 A2 | |
| Wellington St Lwr | 11 B3 | |
| Wellington St Upr | 11 B3 | |
| Wellpark Avenue | 4 D1 | |
| Werburgh Street | 19 B3 | |
| Wesley Place | 27 A2 | |
| West Road | 13 B3 | |
| Western Road | 26 D2 | |
| Western Way | 11 B3 | |
| Westland Row | 21 A3 | |
| Westland Square | 21 A2[6] | |
| Westmoreland St | 20 C2 | |
| Wexford Street | 28 C1 | |
| Whelan House | 22 D3[10] | |
| Whitebank Road | 23 B3 | |
| Whitefriar Gardens | 19 B3[13] | |
| Whitefriar Place | 20 C3[9] | |
| Whitefriar Street | 19 B3 | |
| Whitehall | 5 A1 | |
| Whites Lane North | 11 B3[11] | |
| Whitworth Avenue | 12 D2[2] | |
| Whitworth Parade | 12 C1[4] | |
| Whitworth Place | 12 C1[3] | |
| Whitworth Road | 11 B1 | |
| Whitworth Terrace | 12 D1[3] | |
| Wicklow Street | 20 C3 | |
| Widow's Houses | 19 A3[20] | |
| Wigan Road | 11 B1 | |
| Wilfield | 31 A3 | |
| Wilfield Park | 31 A3 | |
| Wilfield Road | 31 A3 | |
| Willbrook House | 28 D3[6] | |
| William St Nth | 13 A2 | |
| William St Sth | 20 C3 | |
| William's Lane | 20 C1 | |
| William's Pl Lwr | 12 D2[4] | |
| William's Place Sth | 27 B1 | |
| William's Pl Upr | 12 C2[5] | |
| Willie Bermingham Pl | 17 B3[1] | |
| Willowfield | 31 B3 | |
| Wilson Terrace | 19 A3 | |
| Wilson's Terrace | 21 A3[1] | |
| Wilton Court | 29 A2[1] | |
| Wilton Place | 29 A2 | |
| Wilton Terrace | 29 A2 | |

| | | |
|---|---|---|
| Windele Road | 4 C2 | |
| Windmill Lane | 21 A2 | |
| Windmill Road | 25 A3 | |
| Windsor Avenue | 13 B1 | |
| Windsor Place | 28 D1 | |
| Windsor Terrace | 27 B3 | |
| Windsor Villas | 13 B1² | |
| Winetavern Street | 19 B2 | |
| Winton Road | 29 A3 | |
| Wolfe Tone Quay | 18 C2 | |
| Wolfe Tone Street | 19 B1 | |
| Wolseley Street | 27 A2³ | |
| Wood Lane | 18 D2¹ | |
| Wood Quay | 19 B2 | |
| Wood Street | 19 B3 | |
| Woodville Road | 4 C3¹ | |
| Wormwood Gate | 19 A2⁷ | |
| Xavier Road | 13 B2 | |
| Yarnhall Street | 19 B1² | |
| York Road | 22 D2 | |
| York Street | 28 C1 | |
| Zardoz Court | 30 C3⁴ | |
| Zoo Road | 17 A1 | |

LIST OF STREETS
NOT NAMED ON MAP
AND SHOWN BY
SMALL NUMBERS

Page | Grid Ref. | Street Name

| Page | Ref. | No. | Street Name |
|---|---|---|---|
| 1 | A2 | 1 | Cloister Court |
| 1 | B3 | 1 | St Finbarr's Court |
| 2 | D1 | 1 | Bellevue Cottages |
| 2 | D3 | 1 | Coke Ovens Cotts |
| 3 | B2 | 1 | St Ita's Road |
| 4 | C2 | 1 | O'Neachtain Road |
| | | 2 | Vera Terrace |
| 4 | C3 | 1 | Woodville Road |
| 4 | D2 | 1 | Beaucourt |
| 4 | D3 | 1 | Edgewood |
| | | 2 | Clonturk Gardens |
| | | 3 | Ivetta Terrace |
| 5 | B2 | 1 | Morrogh Road |
| | | 2 | Torlogh Parade |
| 6 | C2 | 1 | St Vincent's Court |
| 6 | D2 | 1 | St John's Court |
| | | 2 | Cherrymount Grove |
| | | 3 | Cherrymount Cres |
| 7 | B2 | 1 | Quarry Cottages |
| 8 | D3 | 1 | Duncan Court |
| 9 | A2 | 1 | Parkview Court |
| 10 | C3 | 1 | Ashford Place |
| | | 2 | Ashford Cottages |
| 10 | D1 | 1 | Fertullagh Road |
| 10 | D3 | 1 | Aughrim Villas |
| | | 2 | St Joseph's Court |
| | | 3 | Kings Court |
| | | 4 | Aughrim Court |
| | | 5 | Shea's Court |
| 11 | A1 | 1 | Connaught Parade |
| 11 | A2 | 1 | Castle Terrace |
| 11 | A3 | 1 | Orchard View |
| | | 2 | Grangegorman Villas |
| 11 | B2 | 1 | Library View Tce |
| | | 2 | St Peter's Court |
| | | 3 | Lynch's Place |
| | | 4 | Weaver Lane |
| | | 5 | Kelly's Lane |
| | | 6 | Phibsborough Place |
| | | 7 | Aranmore Avenue |
| | | 8 | St Vincent St Nth |
| | | 9 | Sarsfield Street |
| | | 10 | Bective Square |
| | | 11 | Royal Canal Court |
| | | 12 | George's Wharf |
| | | 13 | Blessington Place |
| 11 | B3 | 1 | St Patrick's Place |
| | | 2 | St Laurence Place |
| | | 3 | Primrose Street |
| | | 4 | Wellington Pl Nth |
| | | 5 | Graham's Row |
| | | 6 | St Mary's Ave Nth |
| | | 7 | Blessington Court |
| | | 8 | St Joseph's Place |
| | | 9 | Mountjoy St Middle |
| | | 10 | Temple Buildings |
| | | 11 | White's Lane North |
| | | 12 | Broadstone Avenue |
| | | 13 | Kings Inn Court |
| | | 14 | Mauncell Place |
| | | 15 | St Michael's Place |
| | | 16 | Delvin Terrace |
| 12 | C1 | 1 | St Alphonsus Ave |
| | | 2 | St Clement's Road |
| | | 3 | Whitworth Place |
| | | 4 | Whitworth Parade |
| 12 | C2 | 1 | Kenmare Parade |
| | | 2 | Muckross Parade |
| | | 3 | Derrynane Parade |
| | | 4 | St Benedict's Gdns |
| | | 5 | Williams Place Upr |
| | | 6 | Sherrard Court |
| | | 7 | St Joseph's Street |
| | | 8 | Synnott Row |
| | | 9 | De Valera Place |
| | | 10 | Josephine Avenue |
| | | 11 | Leo Avenue |
| | | 12 | George's Place |
| 12 | C3 | 1 | St Anthony's Place |
| | | 2 | Hardwicke Arch |
| | | 3 | Hardwicke Lane |
| | | 4 | Frederick Court |
| | | 5 | Gardiner Row |
| | | 6 | Hardwicke Place |
| | | 7 | Frederick Lane Nth |
| | | 8 | Bethesda Place |
| | | 9 | Cavendish Row |
| | | 10 | Britain Place |
| 12 | D1 | 1 | Robert Place |
| | | 2 | St Patrick's Terrace (Fitzroy Ave) |
| | | 3 | Whitworth Terrace |
| 12 | D2 | 1 | Drumcondra Park |
| | | 2 | Whitworth Avenue |
| | | 3 | Portland Court |
| | | 4 | William's Place Lwr |
| | | 5 | Belvidere Avenue |
| | | 6 | Campbell's Lane |
| | | 7 | Campbell's Row |
| | | 8 | Portland Square |
| | | 9 | St Patrick's Tce (Russell St) |
| | | 10 | Wellesley Place |
| | | 11 | St Margaret's Ave Nth |
| | | 12 | Richmond Lane |
| | | 13 | St Joseph's Tce (N.C.Rd) |
| | | 14 | Mountjoy Parade |
| | | 15 | Tyrrell's Place |
| | | 16 | Brendan Behan Ct |
| 12 | D3 | 1 | Matt Talbot Court |
| | | 2 | Simmon's Place |
| | | 3 | Thompson's Cotts |
| | | 4 | Rutland Cottages |
| | | 5 | Terrace Place |
| | | 6 | Bella Place |
| | | 7 | Bella Avenue |
| | | 8 | Gloucester Lane |
| | | 9 | Gloucester Pl Lwr |
| | | 10 | St Mary's Mansions |
| | | 11 | Liberty House |
| | | 12 | Buckingham Village |
| | | 13 | Gloucester Diamond |
| | | 14 | Lourdes House |
| | | 15 | Langrishe Place |
| | | 16 | Belmont Place |
| | | 17 | Father Scully House |
| | | 18 | Mountain View Ct |
| | | 19 | Avondale House |
| 13 | A1 | 1 | Tom Clarke House |
| 13 | A2 | 1 | Sackville Gardens |

19 B3 1 St Francis Square
2 Davis Place
3 Schoolhouse La W
4 St Audoen's Terrace
5 Borris Court
6 John Field Road
7 Longford St Great
8 St Michael's Hill
9 Christchurch Sq
10 St Michael's Close
11 Iveagh Bldgs
(Bride St)
12 Lord Edward Court
13 Whitefriar Gardens
14 Hanover Court
15 Power's Square
16 Clarence Mangan Sq
17 Bride Close
20 C1 1 Findlater Place
2 Strongs Court
20 C2 1 Litton Lane
2 Abbey Cottages
3 Adair Lane
4 Bedford Row
5 Asdill's Row
6 Merchants Arch
7 Fownes Street Lwr
8 Cecilia Street
9 Crampton Court
10 Parliament Row
11 Champion Quay
12 Palace Street
13 Meetinghouse Square
14 Curved Street
15 Temple Bar Square
20 C3 1 Harry Street
2 Chatham Lane
3 Balfe Street
4 Coppinger Row
5 Chatham Row
6 Clarendon Market
7 Longford Street Little
8 Longford Lane
9 Whitefriar Pl
10 Glendinning Lane
11 St Andrews Lane
12 Johnson Place
13 Clarendon Row
14 Chatham Row
15 Tangier Lane
16 Glovers Court
20 D1 1 Frenchman's Lane
2 Moland Place
3 Spencer Row
4 Marlborough Place

5 Northumberland Sq
6 Deverell Place
7 Talbot Lane
8 Gandon Hall
9 Custom Hall
10 Marlborough Court
20 D2 1 Corn Exchange Pl
2 Rath Row
3 Bracken's Lane
4 Brunswick Villas
5 Cards Lane
6 Leinster Market
20 D3 1 Nassau Place
2 Molesworth Place
3 Kildare Place
21 A2 1 Magennis Square
2 Peterson's Court
3 Lombard Court
4 Trinity Square
5 Countess Markievicz
House
6 Westland Square
21 A3 1 Wilson's Terrace
2 Merrion Close
3 Cumberland Court
4 College Lane
21 B1 1 St Laurence Pl East
2 Blythe Avenue

21 B3 1 Island Villa
2 Greenore Terrace
3 Rostrevor Terrace
4 Pearse Grove
5 Clanwilliam Square
6 Clanwilliam Terrace
7 Hogan Place
8 Albert Place East
9 Conway Court
22 C1 1 Carbury Terrace
2 Irvine Cottages
3 Church Place
4 Church Avenue
5 Church Row
22 C3 1 Ormeau Street
2 Waterside Flats
3 The Anchorage
22 D2 1 Fisherman's Wharf
2 Alexandra Quay
3 Cambridge Square
22 D3 1 Cambridge Court
2 Canon Mooney Gdns
3 Parkview Place
4 Herbert Place
5 Philomena Terrace

6 Veronica Terrace
7 Magdalen Terrace
8 Strasburg Terrace
9 Tyrrel's Place
10 Whelan House
11 O'Rahilly House
12 St Joseph's Tce
13 Victoria Cottages
14 St Mary's Terrace
(Ringsend)
15 Seapoint Terrace
16 Simpson's Lane
17 George Reynolds Flats
23 A3 1 Kyle-Clare Road
25 A1 1 Hybreasal
2 The Paddock
25 B1 1 Almeida Terrace
25 B3 1 Moracrete Cottages
26 C1 1 McCarthy Terrace
2 Colbert's Fort
3 Fatima Mansions
4 Rialto Place
5 Boardman's Lane
26 D1 1 St Margaret's Ave
2 Huxley Crescent
3 Spencer Terrace
4 Brandon Terrace
5 Our Lady's Close
26 D2 1 Priestfield Cottages
2 Priestfield Drive
3 Ellford Terrace
27 A1 1 St John's Street
2 Warrenmount Place
3 Geoffrey Keating Rd
4 Cow Parlour
5 O'Curry Avenue
6 Watkin's Buildings
7 Weaver's Close
8 Brabazon Place
9 Warrenmount
10 Weaver's Square
27 A2 1 St Greenville Parade
2 Sandford Park
3 Wolseley Street
4 Brainsboro Terrace
5 Griffith Square
6 Garden Terrace
7 Greenville
27 A3 1 Hatters Lane
2 Greenmount Square
3 Armstrong Street
4 Le Vere Terrace
5 Harold's Cross Cotts
27 B1 1 Old Mill Court
2 St Kevins Avenue